Deborah
Champaign 1983

Proceedings of the 1976 Clinic on Library Applications of Data Processing: The Economics of Library Automation

Papers presented at the
1976 Clinic on Library Applications
of Data Processing, April 25-28, 1976

The Economics of Library Automation

Edited by
J. L. DIVILBISS

University of Illinois
Graduate School of Library Science
Urbana-Champaign, Illinois

LC Card Number: 77-075153
ISBN: 0-87845-046-7
U.S. ISSN: 0069-4789

TABLE OF CONTENTS

INTRODUCTION

The Thirteenth Annual Clinic on Library Applications of Data Processing was held at the Illini Union on the campus of the University of Illinois, April 25-28, 1976. The 1976 clinic had as its theme the economics of library automation, a topic of increasing importance to librarians as they cope with inflation and other financial problems. In planning the clinic we attempted to cover many different aspects of a complex and difficult area. Some of the papers deal with fairly specific library processes, such as circulation or book catalog production, while others deal with more general techniques for determining costs and benefits. The paper by Veneziano and Aagaard is a particularly lucid study of the economics of independent, rather than cooperative, development. They use their own library as an example, but the implications of their work extend far beyond Northwestern University Library. In his paper, Gorman argues persuasively that an activity as mundane as data entry can and should involve sophisticated analysis and planning. In a somewhat speculative vein, Folk takes us into the near future when scholarly journals will exist only as on-line computer files, thus saving the librarians from checking in and shelving low-demand materials. In none of the papers are there formulas for magically reducing the expense of automation. There are, however, serious and intelligent suggestions for dealing with the inescapable problems of cost and value.

J. L. DIVILBISS
Editor

FREDERICK G. KILGOUR
Executive Director
Ohio College Library Center

Economics of Library Computerization

In talking about the economics of library computerization I will answer the question: What is meant by the economics of library computerization? The economics that I am concerned with is scientific economics, the study of how men in society elect to use limited resources for the production of goods and services. The three fundamental economic questions in any society are: What is to be produced? How is it to be produced? For whom is it to be produced? The same questions apply to librarianship and to library computerization.

The major publication on library economics is *Economics of Academic Libraries* by William J. Baumol and Matityahu Marcus,[1] with which I presume most of you here are familiar. The word *academic* appears in the title because the authors' data came from academic libraries; however, their findings are valid for public libraries, school libraries, and special libraries. Per unit costs in academic libraries were rising at a rate of about 6.3 percent per year for the two decades following 1950. This increase can be compared to a 0.9 percent per year rise in the wholesale price index. From this comparison it is obvious that libraries are headed for serious trouble. Baumol and Marcus concluded, very rightly, that some profound modification in the manner in which libraries operate is going to have to occur in the relatively near future. A 6.3 percent annual rate of increase means that in twenty-five years, per unit costs of service will increase by 460 percent. This is the kind of increase that society apparently will not support and, as you know, we are already experiencing diminishing financial support in librarianship. Major changes must occur in what is produced or how it is produced and for whom—possibly in all three. My remarks will be concerned with how computerization can, and does, have a profound impact on these three fundamental questions.

Baumol and Marcus make the interesting point that the cost of computerization had been declining at a rate of 55 percent per year, going in the opposite direction from costs in libraries, and far more precipitously. The reason that costs go up so rapidly in libraries is that libraries are highly labor-intensive. Library salaries are forced up by salary increases in other sectors of the economy, but in the case of libraries these salary increases are not accompanied by increased productivity. This situation is not unique to librarianship; it is also true of education, hospitals, artistic performances, restaurants and many other labor-intensive activities. When Baumol and Marcus analyzed the economic variables within library operations and correlated them, it was abundantly clear that libraries are labor-intensive service institutions, and it is this factor that leads to the disproportionate rate of rise of per unit costs. It is unit costs that must be considered if useful comparisons are to be made.

Another important conclusion made by Baumol and Marcus was that increased costs were not due to inefficiencies in library operation, nor were they caused by mismanagement as is sometimes alleged. Actually, efficiencies in libraries seem to be extraordinarily high. Librarians have been able to achieve something of great significance in that they employ techniques of mass production for products which are all different. Mass production is clearly efficient when large numbers of identical items are produced, but this isn't the case for individual books coming out of the processing line. Nevertheless, librarians have adapted the technique of mass production to the processing of totally unlike individual products, one of the major advances to have occurred in libraries in the last forty to fifty years.

Even though libraries operate efficiently, studies of libraries show that libraries are in failure. Studies in both academic libraries and public libraries have shown that approximately 50-60 percent of the time, a user does not get the information he wants.[2] This failure rate is too high; it turns people away from libraries, and it has turned me away from libraries; I no longer have the time to experience a 50 percent failure rate. I used to publish a fair amount of material in the history of science and the history of technology, but I no longer do so because it takes too much time to get the data. There are just too many interesting scholarly questions that are easier to answer without spending time using a big library.

A general rule of economics applicable to many commodities is that as a price of a good is raised, the demand for the good declines. We see something of this sort occurring in libraries, where as the cost to users to use libraries increases, demand by users decreases. Cost to the user is, of course, generally measured in time, and we all know of cases where the user's cost was too great. For example, a professor of political science at Yale University (where I was associated with the library) had a sabbatical to write a book, but was making such slow progress using the huge Yale library that he went to Geneva to the ILO library, where he finished rapidly using a much smaller library which had information more readily available. I have had some experience in writing a book using the Yale library, and it was hard work even twenty years ago.

In an interesting recent paper,[3] Raymond Jackson uses a mathematical model to show that as the use of a library increases, the book stock erodes, and the only way to continue good service is to limit the service of the library. I can give you an interesting example of this kind of observation from my own experience. Nearly forty years ago, when I was at the Harvard College Library, I observed something curious in the figures for the number of borrowers and the amount of total circulation. I did a correlation between the number of registered borrowers (one had to register in those days to be a borrower) and the total circulation over a period of fifteen to twenty years for which figures were available. There was an inverted ratio; that is to say, the fewer people registered to use the library, the greater the total amount of circulation—except for two years. I was so intrigued that there were two years which didn't fit that I went back to the original records of circulation for those two years, did the additions again, and after having corrected the figures, the two years did follow the pattern.

I certainly would not advocate that the only way to improve service in libraries is to limit service per individual user or to limit the number of users. If we are to reverse the rate-of-failure trend, we are going to have to increase availability of information. Now the information may be in the library and inaccessible or it may be that it is not in the library. With some exceptions, as libraries grow larger they become more and more passive in their services. They don't actively serve their users; they don't really participate in their users' programs. There is an increasing need for libraries to offer services actively if they are to pull out of failure. The major general change must be from a passive service to an active service in terms of what is going to be produced, how it is going to be produced, by whom, and what technology is to be used.

To what extent will libraries support information needs and to what extent will publishers fill the need? The people who use libraries also buy books, and in recent years we have had considerable evidence that an increasing amount of information is coming from publishers rather than from libraries. The "for whom" question means that it is necessary to define the community of users, and just saying "all people in the United States" is not enough. There must be a more useful definition. Most of us talk in the terms of "all" and the National Commission on Library and Information Science talks in terms of "all," but we know very well that not all people are served and not all people even want to use libraries. But how does one define "users" more accurately to make the correct economic moves to answer this extremely important question?

In connection with each of these questions, we must reexamine the objectives of libraries. How are you going to increase the supply? How are you going to make more information available? And, once again, for whom are you going to make it available? For example, it is technically possible to connect a cable television system to a network computer so that anyone with a television set on the cable system could access the catalog in the network computer, but such an arrangement still leaves the question of for whom the service would be provided. Not everybody has a television set on a cable system, and moreover, there are only one hundred communities in the United States with cable television systems capable of supporting two-way communication. Catalog access through cable television is clearly a worthwhile service, but one that can not be provided to all potential users.

It seems to me that Baumol and Marcus are absolutely correct when they say that some profound modification has to be made in library operation—which means that library service cannot be substantially improved by traditional means. In making a profound modification, the technology of choice is obviously an information processing machine: the computer. Computer technology is the only technology available that can greatly enhance productivity of library staff. The computer as a labor-saving device can be thought of as a logical extension of the technique of mass production with interchangeable parts developed in the United States in the second quarter of the nineteenth century. Such production greatly changed the economic aspects of industrialization and also made possible the production of new products. Mass production using interchangeable parts was developed in clock manufacture and in armories in the United States. The original objective of the manufacture of muskets with interchangeable parts was that weapons could be repaired in the field without having a hoard of armorers with forges accompanying an army. It turned out that this technique also had an enormous economic power, although this was not realized until it was employed commercially. A good example of the use of mass production in the commercial sector was the manufacture of the Colt revolver, which could not have been produced as a commercial success without this new technology.

Some of the labor-saving principles that computerization can make are: (1) an increase in work done mechanically, (2) computers permit nonhuman sources of power to be substituted for human effort, (3) high volume of output, (4) high operating speed, (5) increased mechanical continuity in operations, and (6) computers permit automatic error detection. Computerization makes it possible for libraries to take advantage of labor-saving principles. These principles alone will increase productivity of staff, but there has to be a continual increase in productivity of the kind seen since the advent of the computer in agriculture, manufacturing, and in service industries.

The second way in which library productivity can be increased is through economies of scale. Here, although an individual library can certainly utilize labor-saving principles, it is really only by networking that economies of scale can be realized to any large extent.[4] I will talk only about shared cataloging, although sharing of computers, programs, and intellectual contributions can result in economies of scale for other library activities. When the Ohio College Library Center (OCLC) first began to operate in 1971, 68 percent of the cataloging done through the system was done using records that were already in the system; now it is 91 percent. This increasing economy of scale certainly yields an increase in productivity, and it is this type of productivity that is so important. If productivity can increase at the same rate as salaries and wages, then libraries will be behaving as the average of institutions and organizations in the economy as a whole. This goal is the one we must strive to attain.

What can the effect of computerization be on objectives? First, it can certainly increase the availability of resources within libraries by greatly enhancing access points to information in a library. Access points are severely limited in card catalogs and in printed book-form catalogs. The first move should be to make information in the library increasingly available.

The second objective is to make resources available outside of the local library, and to do so networking is, of course, required. There have been some very interesting developments in this area, particularly in that smaller libraries are now making their resources available in a way that was impossible before networks were developed. We have never had a precise concept of a national library in the United States, and we certainly don't mean by a national library what is meant in Spain, for example. With networks the national library will be made up of the nation's libraries, not any particular library. Individual libraries such as the Library of Congress certainly have unique contributions to make, but we can no longer look at any single library as being the pinnacle or hub of library resources. Clearly, the existence of a distributed national library can only be achieved with a computerized network.

The third objective is to enable libraries to take a more active stance in providing services. It is difficult to see how a more active stance can be achieved in larger libraries without the use of computers. An example of such a new service is selective dissemination of information (SDI), and those of you who are recipients of an SDI service know how extremely helpful such a service can be. The on-line catalog is another example of both a new product and an important new service.[5] It is new because on-line catalogs are entirely different in design from card catalogs or printed book catalogs; they are neither on-line card catalogs nor on-line printed book catalogs. They are, instead, huge numbers of miniature catalogs. The OCLC system at present has somewhat more than 1.5 million of these "minicats" in the system with no catalog, as presented to a user, having more than 32 entries. Complex cataloging rules have been a natural consequence of increasing catalog size, but with a catalog of no more than thirty-two entries, there is no need for the complexity of the *Anglo-American Cataloging Rules*. Certainly, rules will be needed, but they should not be based on bibliographic principles; rather, rules should be based on users' requirements of catalogs. Recognition and acceptance of the concept of miniature catalogs will lead to one of the most profound modifications that will occur in librarianship, namely, mechanized descriptive cataloging. There does not appear to be any reason why descriptive cataloging could not be done largely in a mechanical way. It will require some human intervention, of course, but when a catalog has no more than thirty-two entries, the entries need not have the requirements for uniqueness and specificity necessary for book-form and card catalogs.[6] Mechanization of descriptive cataloging is only one of the ways in which computerization will affect the economies of libraries, and is also an example of the profound changes that the Baumol and Marcus study revealed as necessary.

What effect will computerization have on the economics of library use? Users are not included in library budgets, and there is a tendency to ignore them from the viewpoint of costs they incur in using a library. Sometimes I wonder just how much computerization is being done to benefit libraries rather than library users. Yet, it should be the users who come first. Their costs are real, and it is a rise in those costs that lead them to discontinue using libraries. Computerization should lower the real cost to users and thereby increase demand for library service. Computerization can certainly bring back to libraries those people for whom the cost of library use has become too great. A study of the Lockheed on-line system in four public libraries in California showed that users of that service were "not the traditional patrons of the public library."[7]

There will also be new users when remote catalog access, such as that at the Ohio State University Libraries and which Thorson discusses in another paper, becomes available, including some users who won't need to go to the library because they will have access through television connection. One of the sinful things about a card catalog is that there is only one of them and you must go to the library to use it. I can assure you that not having to go to a library is a very important improvement in providing library service. I didn't use the Ohio State University (OSU) library to any extent prior to the adoption of this sytem because I wasn't prepared to spend a half-day going to and from the library and perhaps having to go to one or two department libraries—only to find that I couldn't get a book. I am prepared to spend the half-minute that it now takes, and the result is that I use two or three times as many books from the OSU library as I did before, and I buy fewer books. OCLC has done a study of public service terminals on the OCLC system and more than four-fifths of the users in both academic and public libraries preferred to use a terminal rather than a card catalog.

In summary, it is all too clear from economic analysis that libraries have extremely serious problems to be solved. There is no way that society is going to support a 460 percent increase in financial support for an institution experiencing a 50-60 percent failure rate in service. Libraries are as efficient as other labor-intensive service industries, and it is impossible to see how any further increase in the efficiency of an already highly efficient operation can cope with such rocketing increases in costs. It is inevitable that a drastic change must occur in library operations; for the immediate future, the greatest desirable impact will come from computerized, on-line networking, that provides not only labor-saving functions but also effective economies of scale.

REFERENCES

1. Baumol, William J., and Marcus, Matityahu. *Economics of Academic Libraries*. Washington, D.C., American Council on Education, 1973.

2. Bundy, Mary Lee. *Metropolitan Public Library Users*. College Park, Md., University of Maryland, School of Library and Information Services, 1968, p. 46; Trueswell, Richard W. "A Quantitative Measure of User Circulation Requirements and its Possible Effect on Stack Thinning and Multiple Copy Determination," *American Documentation* 16:22, Jan. 1965; and Buckland, Michael K. *Book Availability and the Library User*. New York, Pergamon Press, 1975, pp. 97, 130.

3. Jackson, Raymond. "Evidence on Erosion of a Resource due to Population Growth: Case of the Public Library," *Land Economics* 50:70-75, Feb. 1974.

4. Kilgour, Frederick G. "Design of On-line Catalogs." *In* ALA Information Science and Automation Division. *The Catalog—Its Nature and Prospects* (ISAD Institute). (In press.)

6. *Ibid.*

7. Ahlgren, A.E. *On-line Search Services in the Public Library: Project Dialib*. Stanford, Calif., Applied Communication Research, 1975, p. 4.

RYBURN M. ROSS
Assistant Director for Technical and Automated Services
Cornell University Libraries
Ithaca, New York

Cost Analysis of Automation in Technical Services

This paper has several purposes: (1) to determine the relationship of automation costs of technical services in a large research library to the total library resource allocations; (2) to describe Cornell University Libraries' history of automation efforts and the accompanying cost experiences; (3) to review a specific cost analysis for processing monographs in a large technical services group; (4) to review productivity measurement of library staff involved in processing; and (5) to propose some general management planning information techniques to measure the performance of technical services staff.

Adequate cost analysis and true determination of costs in technical services has always been a very elusive matter. Although there have been numerous feasibility studies performed on various processing centers and technical processes, few such studies have been followed by thorough cost studies after new automated library systems were installed. In addition, the techniques for performing such studies have varied so widely that comparisons of studies are rarely valid. Perhaps the best that any library can hope for is that it will continually study its own processes and their costs and base management conclusions on this information without attempting to make comparative studies with other libraries.

In 1967, Paul Fasana made the following points concerning the determination of library automation costs: (1) few factual data exist on this topic; (2) library automation is expensive; (3) considerable conjecture is centered on the anticipated efficiencies and savings once computer-based systems are designed and implemented; (4) cost figures in themselves are meaningless; and (5) determination of the cost of automated library procedures is needed.[1]

Unfortunately, almost a decade has passed with little progress made in an area of library management so vital to a library's total resource allocation. A greater portion of each large research library's budget, hard hit by annual inflationary forces, is being expended for automation. Initially, the purpose of implementing automated systems was to lower unit costs, particularly in the book processing areas of the library. More recently, library managers have justified the installation of automated library systems by citing such factors as improved service to the library patrons and reduced processing times. Today, less emphasis is placed on cost reductions achieved by using computers to perform clerical tasks in libraries.

Library Resource Allocation

Although there is little hard data on amounts spent by libraries on automation, Brett Butler estimates that "somewhat less than five percent of overall budgets go to automated service costs."[2] He also points out that very few libraries were involved in automation activities ten years ago, but now almost every library is involved in some form of automated activity, "even if they only buy catalog cards which are generated by computerized systems." Butler now estimates that from $125 to $175 million is now spent annually on various automated systems and activities and that within the next eight years, these same expenditures will approach $400-$500 million and comprise 8-15 percent of the libraries' budgets. In the future such extensive expenditures will require detailed cost analyses and careful reallocation of library resources. Such resources are already burdened by tremendous pressures to maintain book collections and install new library programs (e.g., audiovisual centers).

The graph used in Figure 1, "Cornell University Libraries, 1974/75 Expenditures by Program," is an excellent method illustrating the various library expenditures by program. One is immediately aware that libraries are highly labor-intensive organizations with large portions of the budget going to staffing the library, processing materials and collection development. Purchase of books and periodicals and preservation of the collection make up nearly the entire remainder of the budget. Cornell University Libraries has proceeded carefully and deliberately in utilizing automation techniques and current operations and processes absorb only a total of $138,947 or 3.2 percent of the total endowed budget. It is expected that this amount will gradually increase each year until approximately 8-10 percent is expended in this program area. Automation costs should be related to the total operating resources of a library system, and because they compete directly with the requirements for staffing and book expenditures, these programs will by necessity require substantial justification. In comparing the Cornell University Libraries' program expenditures with another large academic research library such as Stanford University Libraries, one is struck by the similarity of the two libraries' program costs with the exception of automation. Due undoubtedly to the fact that the BALLOTS system is now operational, the percentage of projected cost for automation in the Stanford library in 1975/76 is 9.6 percent of the total budget.[3]

Cornell University Libraries Initial Automation Plans

In 1965 Cornell University Libraries employed a systems analyst to study the application of computers and data processing techniques to various library operations. After several months of study and consultation with experts, a 5-year library automation program was established. This program called for the automation of three basic library processes: (1) monographic acquisitions, (2) serial records control, and (3) circulation and inventory control.[4] All of these procedures require numerous repetitive clerical tasks which appeared well suited to data processing methods and equipment. As part of this initial study, a mathematical model was constructed which plotted the "Systems Costs vs. Time" for the manual systems, improved manual systems and envisioned automated systems (see Figure 2). Every effort was made to incorporate all direct and indirect costs in all three systems, including salary increases to cover the annual inflation factor. In determining the costs for the improved manual systems, sufficient clerical labor was added to the existing staff to maintain all processes on a current basis. However, in this estimate no attempt was made to add the additional labor required to provide the same level of services expected of the automated systems. Figure 2 illustrates that more than five years elapses before costs of development and implementation are recovered.

At the time of the study it was estimated that approximately $250,000 would be needed to develop all three computerized systems. In 1966, the university administration gave the libraries a small grant to begin work on the first system, later to be called the Automated Acquisitions and In-Process Control System. The acquisitions system became operational in January 1968 and is a series of computer programs which handle the majority of routine work for the centralized Acquisitions Department. This department orders and receives monographic material for ten separate college libraries on campus. The system performs approximately sixty-five various operations involved in ordering, receiving, bookkeeping, and generating management information and statistical reports. The receiving system records the in-process status of material, initiates the automatic claiming and cancellation processes, and posts charges to more than 300 accounts. The system provides an on-order and in-process weekly status report in alpha main entry sequence to be used by searchers and the public services departments. Over 32,000 titles are represented in the main status list. "Mini-Master" lists showing the status of acquisitions for each individual college and departmental library are made available through a computer-sort routine. A unique feature of this system is that monographic series titles are accommodated both by author-title entry in

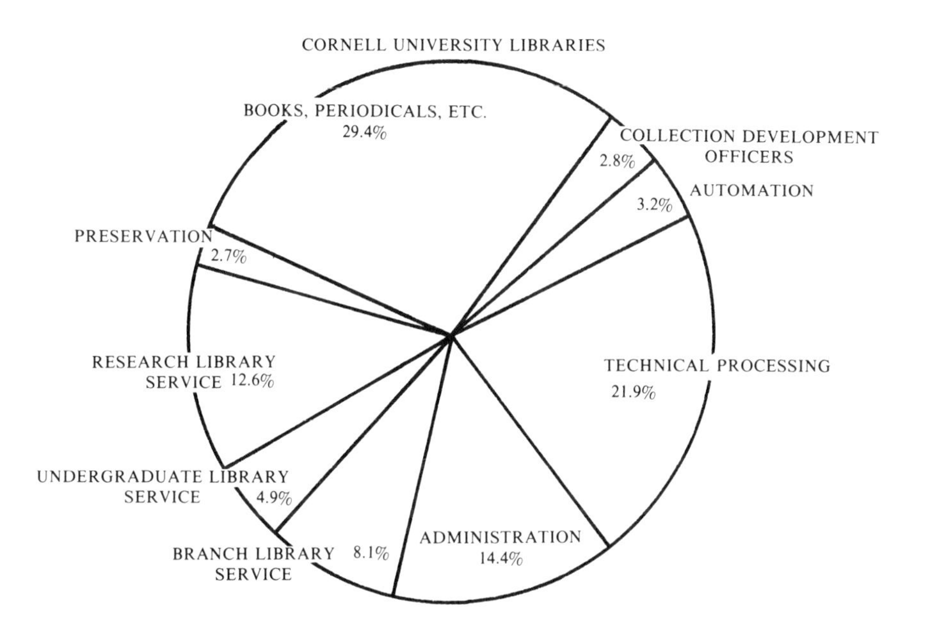

1974/75 Expenditures By Program
(endowed divisions excluding the Law Library)

Books, Periodicals, Etc.	$1,278,076	29.4%
Preservation (Binding)	$ 118,474	2.7%
Research Library Service	$ 547,381	12.6%
Undergraduate Library Service	$ 214,122	4.9%
Branch Libraries Service	$ 350,217	8.1%
Administration (Incl. General Expenses)	$ 627,716	14.4%
Technical Processing	$ 954,433	21.9%
Automation	$ 138,947	3.2%
Collection Development Officers	$ 121,192	2.8%
Total	$4,350,558	100.0%

Figure 1. Cornell University Libraries, 1974/75 expenditures by program

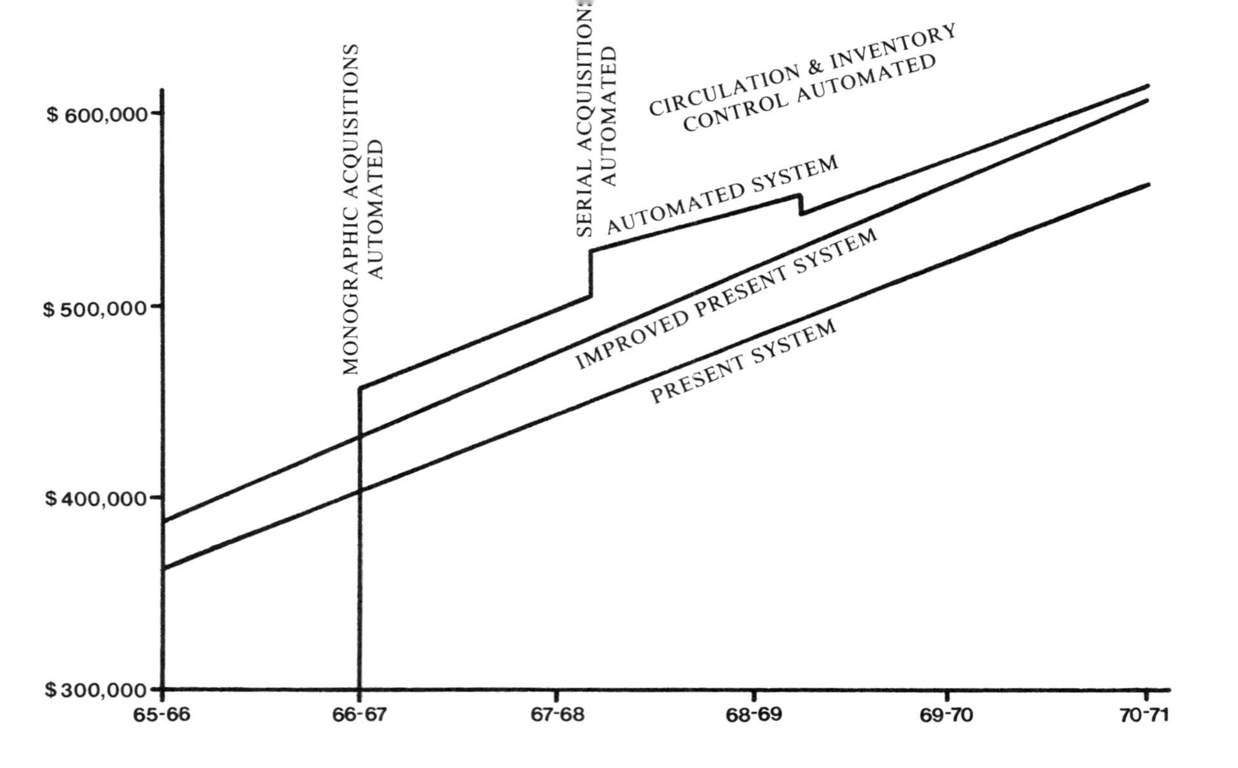

Figure 2. Systems cost vs. time; Total Cost Less Overhead For: 1 Monographic Acq., 2 Serial Acq., 3 Circulation

Source: Blakely, Robert. "Projected Automated Costs for 1) Monographic Acquisitions, 2) Serials Acquisition, 3) Circulation and Inventory Control; FY 66-67." October 1975. (Unpublished report.)

the main status list and in quarterly listing by series entry for approximately 10,000 standing orders.

A summary of the total development costs, production cost history and detailed production costs for FY 1974/75 is given in Table 1. The initial development cost of $87,594 was approximately what the libraries had expected. However, production costs from the initial feasibility estimate of $12,000 above the then-current labor costs increased annually until in FY 1972/73 it totaled $72,760. Each year during the period 1968/69-1972/73 the production cost for this system exceeded its budget despite all efforts by the libraries and the Office of Computer Services to project budgeted amounts and hold costs down. Contributing factors behind this frustrating rise in charges are outlined as follows. The system was developed on an IBM/360 Model 40 with a price quotation of $50 per CPU hour. The following year a larger computer (IBM/360 Model 65) was installed in the central computer center in support of the university's administrative, academic and research computing needs. A priority system for utilizing the computer was also instituted at that time. In order for the libraries' acquisitions system to be processed on a weekly schedule, Priority 8 (the highest priority utilized for administrative production runs) was required. This priority level carried with it a cost of $300 per CPU hour, which is a 600 percent increase over the previous rate.

In subsequent years the cost per hour for computer time increased almost annually and even though the library was able to lower the priority rate to six, production costs continued to increase. Finally, in FY 1973/74 the Office of Computer Services agreed to run portions of this system at a lower priority (five) and budget projections were met. In 1974 the Office of Computer Services installed an IBM/370 Model 168 and, even though this computer ran five times faster than the IBM/360 Model 65, costs remained the same. When the director of the Office of Computer Services was asked why the production costs for the acquisitions system did not decrease, he responded by writing:

> Please beware that there are three parameters to consider—charges (costs), service and resources. A true cost saving is one which reduces the use of resources (computing and staff time, supplies, etc.) while maintaining service. A cost saving which reduces charges by use of lower priorities (no saving in computing resources) cannot lead to maintaining services. Your risk, in this case, is possible delays in delivery of output as a tradeoff on the effect on us which is reduced income for the same use of high cost computing resources.

It is obvious that the university's cost increase in hardware and operation software enhancement over this 7-year period did nothing to reduce total library costs; rather they increased dramatically. The lesson to be learned here is that bigger and better computers do not mean lower production costs.

Initial Development Costs

System Design, Programming & Testing	$ 75,000
Supplies (Initial Quantities)	3,658
Equipment Purchased	500
Manual Labor--Change-over & To Run Down Old OOF	8,436
Total Initial Development Costs	$ 87,594

Production Costs History

	Year	*Cost*	*Priority*	*Computer Cost/Hr.*	*Computer*
Feasibility Estimate	1967/68	$12,000		$ 50	IBM360/40
Initial Production (6 Mo.)	1968/69	$18,036	8	$300	IBM360/65
Full Production	1969/70	$31,000	8	$300	IBM360/65
Full Production	1970/71	$59,098	6	$375	IBM360/65
Full Production	1971/72	$66,075	6	$400	IBM360/65
Full Production	1972/73	$72,760	6	$400	IBM360/65
Full Production	1973/74	$64,941	5&6	$280 & $400	IBM360/65
Full Production	1974/75	$66,077	5&6	$280 & $400	IBM 370/168

Production Costs 1974/75	*Cost*	*% Of Total Cost*
Computers		
370/168	$31,663	47.9%
360/20	9,545	14.4%
Total	$41,208	62.4
Forms	14,885	22.5
Keypunch Rental	4,025	6.1
Controller	3,900	5.9
File Rental/Storage	2,059	3.1
Total Production Costs	$66,077	100.0

Table 1. Automated Acquisitions and In-Process Control System

Progress toward achieving the initial goals of the 5-year plan was considerably slower than what the libraries had programmed. This was due mainly to such factors as the need for extensive and detailed systems analysis, unavailable funds necessary for programmers, lack of trained data processing personnel familiar with library processes, delays in obtaining the necessary computer time for testing purposes, frequent computer configuration and operating system changes, and the necessity at all times of maintaining normal daily operations.

An analysis of production costs (Table 1) for the automated acquisition system indicates that approximately 77.5 percent of the total annual costs for this system is paid out for computer time, keypunch machine rentals, computer controller, computer file rental and storage. This leaves only 22.5 percent of the production costs with which to attempt further reductions. Batch process systems are notorious paper generators and this fact, coupled with increasing paper costs, means that additional savings can be made if a suitable substitute can be found for the paper output. We have concentrated our most recent efforts in this cost area. A substitute was sought in the form of Computer Output Microfilm (COM) for the paper products. A recent cost comparison of the printed lists versus COM output indicates that approximately $7,500 per year can be saved after the initial investment in microfiche readers. The library has decided to go to a COM output for the status list in the next fiscal year, thus taking advantage of the additional saving.

Once the COM system is implemented, it is doubtful that anything more will be done to enhance this rather obsolete acquisitions system. A search is already underway for a substitute which will provide lower production costs, be more flexible in operating, require less in-house maintenance and provide better and more timely products. There are several alternatives to be considered: (1) service from a network such as OCLC; (2) purchase of a commercially available package such as the Baker and Taylor BATAB System; (3) purchase of a turnkey minicomputer system complete with software; or (4) purchase of a minicomputer and acquisition of a necessary transferrable operating system from another university, such as the University of Minnesota Biomedical Library or the University of Chicago. These latter systems are complete library data management systems and encompass many additional library processes.

Network Evolvement

In 1970 the university administration decided that due to fiscal constraint some retrenchment in all academic departments was mandatory. A 3-year program was announced, and it was obvious that additional money to develop in-house library systems would not be forthcoming.

Fortunately, at about the same time, the Ohio College Library Center (OCLC) announced that it would accept additional libraries outside of Ohio as members for access to the on-line Cataloging Support Module if they were members of a consortium. The Cornell University Libraries in conjunction with the other four largest university libraries in central and western New York had formed such a consortium in 1967 called the Five Associated University Libraries (FAUL). The board of directors of this organization recognized the immediate utility of the OCLC Cataloging Support Module, and in two meetings (October 1970 and January 1971) the board approved joining OCLC in a common venture. A feasibility study had been prepared for the board's consideration within this 3-month period by the FAUL Technical Services Committee. The feasibility study[5] indicated that there would be substantial savings in the cataloging processes for all five libraries in utilizing the OCLC on-line cataloging system. Table 2 shows the estimated current manual costs versus the expected future costs for the FAUL libraries.

In addition to contributing to the FAUL feasibility study, the Cornell University Libraries performed additional cost studies[6] in July 1972 (Table 2) prior to the installation of the OCLC Model 100 terminals in October 1973, and again in January 1975[7] in order to try to determine exact cataloging and processing times and costs after installation of the terminals (see Table 3). The long period from July 1972 to January 1975, together with the differing techniques and cost elements, makes comparison of these three studies difficult and nearly meaningless.

Processing Costs, Staff Productivity and Cost Savings

The analysis of processing costs for social science monographs shown in Table 3 is the result of one of the most comprehensive time and cost studies ever completed for a large central technical services operation. An attempt was made to cover all direct and indirect labor costs including benefits, overhead, major supply items and a compensation factor for work efficiency for all staff members included in the study. Also included is a prorated unit cost for both the Automated Acquisitions and In-Process Control System and the OCLC Cataloging Support System. The total cost of $9.86 for processing each monographic title developed in this study is very realistic.

In reviewing this summary analysis, one is immediately aware that the prorated unit costs for the automated systems now absorb approximately thirty percent of all costs and it is in these areas where reductions must be made to further shrink the total processing costs. It would be extremely difficult to reduce the direct labor costs (28.4 percent) and the overhead and fringe benefits (19.2 percent) because these two cost elements continue to rise with the cost of living; the compensating factor for work efficiency (23.4 percent) remains somewhat stable in any work force.

A unique feature of the Bayunus study[8] was the calculation of a compensating factor for work efficiency and the inclusion of this indirect labor cost into the total processing cost figure. The direct labor costs were computed by using productive hours. This was obtained by passing a sample lot of titles through the various work stations in the technical services and by the staff recording "time-worked" notations for the entire lot. A work efficiency factor of .8248 requires that a Productive Time Ratio (PTR) for all staff members be computed. PTR is defined as the fraction of each productive

Feasibility Cost Estimates--FAUL Libraries (1971)

	Current Cost	*Future Cost*
Library No. 1	$ 7.51	$ 4.87
Library No. 2	12.98	5.10
Cornell	8.14	5.33
Library No. 4	6.03	5.03
Library No. 5	9.43	5.11

Cost/Title Summary (July, 1972)

	Unit Orders	*Blanket Orders*
Acquisitions	$ .723	$ .953
Cataloging	1.062	1.728
Card Production	.825	.890
Total Labor Costs	$2.610	$3.571
Overhead (20%)	.522	.714
Equipment (Card Production)	.116	.116
Total Cost/Title	$3.248	$4.401

Table 2. OCLC Cataloging Module Costs

salaried hour. At Cornell a full-time staff member is compensated for 2,028 hours each year. An average of 490 hours of the 2,028 is unavailable for productive labor because of annual leave, personal leave, sick leave, national holidays, and coffee breaks. This leaves 1,538 hours available for productive labor:

$$2{,}028 \text{ hrs.} - 490 \text{ hrs.} = 1{,}538 \text{ hrs.}$$

As a result of this study it was learned that the average worker was engaged in productive effort 72.3 percent of the 1,538 available hours:

$$\text{PTR} = \frac{\text{Productive Hours}}{\text{Salaried Hours}} = \frac{72.3\% \times 1{,}538 \text{ hrs.}}{2{,}028 \text{ hrs.}} = 54.8\%$$

The compensating factor for work efficiency represents the number of nonproductive hours for each productive hour. For every 1,000 hours, 548 will be productive:

$$1{,}000 \text{ hrs.} \times \text{PTR} = 1{,}000 \text{ hrs.} \times .548 = 548 \text{ hrs.}$$

Conversely, for every 1,000 hours, 452 will be nonproductive:

$$1{,}000 \text{ hrs.} - 548 \text{ hrs.} = 452 \text{ hrs.}$$

I. Direct Labor			
A. Measured Labor			
Shipping Room	$0.0202		
Automated Systems Control Group	0.0892		
Acquisitions Department	0.9639		
Catalog Department	1.6563		
Marking & Plating Section	0.0719		
	$2.8015		28.41%
B. Compensating Factor for Work Efficiency			
Measured Labor / Compensating Factor			
$2.8015 X 0.8248 =	$2.3107		23.43%
Total -- Direct Labor		$5.1122	
II. Overhead (21%) and Fringe Benefits (16%)			
Direct Labor / Overhead & Fringes			
$5.1122 X 0.37 =		$1.8915	19.18%
Sub-Total--Direct Labor, Overhead & Fringe Benefits		$7.0037	
III. Materials and Equipment			
Acquisitions Dept. (Xerox Rental, Xerox Paper, Forms)	$0.0208		
Automated Systems Control Group (3-IBM 129's, 1-IBM 059)	0.0751		
Marking & Plating Section (Labels and Bookplates)	0.0140		
Total--Materials and Equipment		$0.1099	01.11%
IV. Acquisitions and In-Process Control System (computer services)		$1.3027	13.21%
V. Cataloging Support System (OCLC)		$1.4439	14.64%
TOTAL COST OF PROCESSING A MONOGRAPH (EXCLUDING BINDING)		$9.8602	

Table 3. Summary of Processing Costs for Social Sciences Monographs

Source: Bayanus, Owais. *A Cost Analysis of the Automated Systems Control Group; The Acquisitions Department and the Catalog Department of the Central Technical Services; Cornell University Libraries.* Jan. 1975. (ED 102 996)

The compensating factor can be computed as follows:

$$\text{Compensating Factor} = \frac{1 - \text{PTR}}{\text{PTR}} = \frac{1 - .548}{.548} = \frac{.452}{.548} = .08248$$

Industry has performed a number of studies on the efficiency of employees in high-volume repetitive office work and has determined that the work is done at 50-60 percent efficiency.[9] The Productive Time Ratio of 54.8 percent found in this study for a large technical services staff concurs with other such studies.

In a paper delivered at the cataloging workshop[10] held in Toronto in June 1975, Elaine Walker, Cornell's Catalog Librarian, estimated that the Catalog and Catalog Maintenance Department required seven fewer librarians and paraprofessional positions after installation of the OCLC Cataloging Support Module, and that two other paraprofessional positions had been downgraded. Three of the released positions were reassigned to other areas of the technical services. The greatest impact on staffing changes came in the catalog maintenance tasks where the staff had been reduced from nineteen in FY 1972/73 to thirteen in FY 1974/75. The entire credit for the staff saving cannot in itself be assigned to the implementation of an automated system; rather, it is the combined effect of reorganizing whole departments, realignment and reassignment of staff and tasks, new patterns of work-flow, new forms and work schedules, stratification of tasks and a careful consideration of requirements of a man-machine environment.

It is estimated, however, that this particular automated cataloging system is now saving the Cornell libraries approximately one dollar per title cataloged on the system. Because the Central Technical Services has been cataloging approximately 45,000 new titles annually since October 1973 on four OCLC Model 100 terminals, it is readily evident that substantial cost benefits have already occurred to the library. In further examination of this data, it should be noted that the amount of direct labor for cataloging presently accounts for only $1.65 of the total processing cost. Additional minor reduction might be made in this cost area, but the total processing cost would obviously not be affected to any great extent.

I am somewhat pessimistic about future savings due to the continuing increases in various cost elements such as the OCLC first-time use charge (utilizing an OCLC record for cataloging purposes), communication charges, terminal maintenance charges, and for the first time, catalog card costs for FY 1976/77. I believe that the OCLC Cataloging Support Module first-time charge is now carrying an inordinate share of the expense for the recent large capital investments in bigger and better computers (Xerox Sigma 9's), systems development and maintenance costs at OCLC. If these cost increases continue beyond the next fiscal year, OCLC will drive many marginally cost-beneficial on-line cataloging operations out of the OCLC system.

Computer Terminal and Cataloging Rates

In determining the total processing costs reported above, valuable data was also obtained regarding computer terminal and cataloging rates utilizing the OCLC Cataloging Support Module (see Table 4). These rates were ascertained when the average response time for the OCLC system was nine seconds or better, and comparable results could only be forthcoming under the same operational conditions.

Prior to the installation of the OCLC system, the library staff decided that for a large operation such as Cornell's it would probably be more efficient to stratify the various tasks to be accomplished. The operation was broken down into the components of searching, cataloging, inputting and proofreading. Various levels of staff were trained in these operations and scheduled for 2-hour shifts on the computer terminals. The searching tasks were assigned to two full-time positions in the Catalog Department, and this personnel accomplished all computer searching as well as any manual searching required in the libraries' union catalog or the National Union Catalog. Cataloging and proofreading tasks were assigned to librarians and paraprofessional catalogers and the inputting tasks were assigned to typists in the Catalog Maintenance Section. This system has worked extremely well—work-flow is smooth and all tasks are usually accomplished on schedule.

The reported searching time of .8 minutes per title includes two researches. At the time of this study, each title was originally searched immediately upon receipt in the Catalog Department. This initial search resulted in locating 65.8 percent of cataloging copy in the data bank. Subsequent researches for remaining titles were made at two 4-week intervals; the second search locating 13.3 percent and the third locating 6.1 percent of cataloging copy. All remaining titles after the 8-week period were sent to the cataloging teams for original cataloging and inputting into the OCLC data bank. The total quantity of cataloging copy located in the OCLC data bank for this social sciences sample lot is substantially higher than for all material cataloged on the OCLC system. In 1974/75 catalog copy (LC MARC and member) was located for 64.7 percent of the 45,642 titles processed on the system. Cornell is currently experiencing a substantial increase in this percentage figure due mainly to increased availability of LC MARC copy for Germanic, Spanish and Portuguese materials as well as additional member copy.

The average cataloging time of 3.96 minutes per title is very similar to that reported in a study of thirty-six Ohio academic libraries which reported an average cataloging time of approximately 4.3 minutes per title.[11] As can be

Terminal Rates (Minutes/Title)			*Cataloging Rates (Minutes/Title)*	
Searching			*LC Copy*	
(Including 2 Researches)		.8	Desk Work	9.66
			Terminal	3.83
				13.49
Cataloging			*Member Copy*	
Average		3.96	Desk Work	14.75
LC Copy	3.83		Terminal	6.18
Member Copy	6.18			
				20.93
Inputting		6.05	*Original*	
			Desk Work	26.26
			Inputting	6.05
			Proofreading	3.05
				35.36
Proofreading		3.05		

Table 4. OCLC Cataloging Support Module

seen from the data in Table 4, there is a substantial difference in the cataloging rates with LC copy (13.49 minutes), member copy (20.93 minutes), and original (35.36 minutes). It is the opinion of Cornell's cataloging staff that original cataloging takes substantially more time than it did with the manual system. Cataloging with member copy takes approximately 50 percent longer than cataloging with LC MARC copy due in large part to variation in entries, nonstandardized subject heading and incomplete cataloging data. Because increasing amounts of member copy are now available through the OCLC system, it is imperative that excellent standards of cataloging be followed by all member libraries and complete MARC records be input into the data bank. In order to bring records below par up to MARC standards, it is suggested that data bank records be edited by regionally located libraries.

Management Data Systems

The cost analysis data which have been discussed in this paper are not in themselves very useful in making rational planning decisions concerning a large technical services operation. Such data must be supported by and utilized in conjunction with other statistical and organizational information in order for the manager to assess past performance effectively and to project future trends in the technical services. A combination of outputs, workloads, backlog counts and processing costs are only a sample of the types of data required for this purpose. Such information should be easily compiled and computed from regularly maintained budget and statistical information. For this purpose the following tables have been found most useful: "Technical Services Cost Ratio" (Table 5), "Cataloging Outputs and Costs" (Table 6), and "Analysis of New Volumes and Titles Cataloged" (Table 7).

The Technical Services Cost Ratio (TSCOR) was developed in the early 1960s by the ALA Resources and Technical Services Division's Technical Services Cost Ratio Committee.[12] It is "a ratio made up of the total cost of technical service salaries divided by the amount spent for library material during a given period of time." The result of this calculation is a decimal form for the amount which it costs in staff salaries to spend one dollar for library materials (books, periodicals and binding). This ratio has been computed annually since the committee issued forms and instructions for computation; Table 5 records TSCOR for the period 1968/69-1974/75 with the exception of 1969/70. The mean professional salaries for each year are also given because this processing cost indicator is certainly susceptible to increases in salaries and the ratio can be expected to change upward by this factor.

One slight variation has been made in the committee's instructions in that, starting in 1970/71, automation acquisition production costs were added into the basic figures on the assumption that such costs should be equated to direct labor costs. In 1973/74, all OCLC production costs for the cataloging module were also added. The resulting rise and decline in the TSCOR ratio since 1970/71 appears to substantiate previously presented production cost data for both automated systems.

As for the utility of this ratio as a measure of a technical services organization's performance, it is believed that a benchmark can be set by the individual libraries in order to judge total achievement. A ratio of less than one for a large research library is a commendable goal. TSCOR is a useful indicator for managers to be aware of and utilize as a performance measure.

Library management often requests information concerning cataloging output, cataloging costs and total volumes, and titles processed. Tables 6 and 7 are compiled annually for this purpose and because they cover more than one year, comparisons can be made and analyzed. Since the OCLC Catalog Support Module was installed in October 1973, it is interesting to note in Table 6 that output per cataloger increased for all three categories: (1) new titles cataloged; (2) new, reclassified and recataloged titles; and (3) new, reclassified and recataloged volumes. This fact is particularly pleasing when one realizes that the cataloging staff had been reduced by almost three full-time equivalent (FTE) catalogers, and yet total outputs were up. Cataloging cost per unit increased slightly but this was due in most part to higher-than-

Technical Services Cost Ratio (TSCOR) is a ratio made up of the total cost of technical services salaries divided by the amount spent for library materials during a given period of time. The figure obtained by putting this ratio in decimal form is the amount it costs in staff salaries to spend one dollar for library materials.

Year	*TSCOR*	*Salary*
1967/68	.749	$ 8,439
1968/69	.75	$ 8,811
1969.70	N.A.	$ 9,132
1970/71	.89*	
1971/72	.96	$10,158
1972/73	.96	$10,168
1973/74	.75**	$11,276
1974/75	.81	$12,382

*Includes Acquisitions and In-Process Control System's costs for the first time.
**Includes OCLC cataloging module's costs for full year.

Table 5. Technical Services Cost Ratio

	1973/74	*1974/75*
Cataloging Positions		
Professional	26.25*	22.50
Paraprofessional	10.00	11.00
Totals	36.25*	33.50*
Salaries		
Professional	$262,358	$278,500
Paraprofessional	65,207	77,835
Totals	$327,565	$356,335
Total Outputs		
New Titles (only)	69,975	70,363
New Titles, Titles Reclass., Titles Recat.	80,975	80,054
New Volumes, Vols. Reclass., Vols. Recat.	120,572	122,274
Cataloging Output Per Cataloger		
New Titles	1930.3	2100.4
New, Reclass., Recat. Titles	2233.8	2389.4
New, Reclass., Recat. Volumes	3326.1	3650.0
Costs		
Per New Title	$4.68	$5.06**
Per Title (new, reclass., recat.)	$4.05	$4.45**
Per Volume (new, reclass., recat.)	$2.71	$2.91**

*Incl. Catalog Librarian, 1/4 Catalog Editor's time, 2.5 Serials Catalogers and their salaries.
**Incl. salary increments given in December, 1974; retroactive to July, 1974.

Table 6. Cataloging Outputs and Costs

Year	Total Staff (FTE)	New Vols. Cataloged	New Titles Cataloged	New Titles Cataloged Per Man Yr.	New Titles Per Man Yr. % of 540.3
1969/70	142.00	132,389	75,004	528	97.7
1970/71	140.00	127,244	75,541	540	99.9
1971/72	137.82	115,130	69,021	501	92.7
1972/73	131.45	123,307	75,005	571	105.7
1973/74	126.65	111,527	69,975	553	102.4
1974/75	128.25	113,241	70,363	549	101.6

1969/70: New Vols Cataloged/New Titles Cataloged = 132,389/75,004 = 1.765
1974/75: New Vols Cataloged/New Titles Cataloged = 113,241/70,363 = 1.609

Table 7. Analysis of New Volumes and Titles Cataloged

normal salary increases given in 1974/75. It is obvious that the implementation of the OCLC Cataloging Support Module has been cost beneficial.

Table 7 attempts to establish a percentage indicator for new titles cataloged per man-year for the entire technical services staff. This analysis is made in order to take into consideration all efforts by the technical services staff in processing new materials. A norm was established by averaging new titles cataloged per man-year and the percentage, as is shown for 1972/73 through 1974/75, has exceeded 100 percent of an established norm. The usefulness of this established norm will be watched carefully in the coming years to see what the future effects will be of: (1) additional on-line processing modules, (2) the increased availability of cataloging copy from LC MARC and OCLC member libraries, (3) the numerous changes in entry rules and subject headings, and (4) the trend to further standardization of cataloging copy.

Future library planning needs the input of timely and useful management data. Library managers need to make concerted and continuing efforts to define the library's objectives to determine adequate performance measures and norms, and to design and implement management information systems in order to accomplish their library's mission in the most cost-beneficial manner possible. Such a system would have the greatest impact on management if the data were automatically collected and analyzed as part of the daily library routines. Unfortunately, no such system exists at this time, and the future prospects for its development look dim. In the meantime, reliance must be made upon such cost analysis and management data as are discussed in this paper.

REFERENCES

1. Fasana, Paul J. "Determining the Cost of Library Automation," *A.L.A. Bulletin* 61:656-61, June 1967.

2. Butler, Brett. "Use of Automated Services," *Bulletin of the American Society for Information Science* 2:21-22, Sept./Oct. 1975.

3. "Selected Facts, Libraries of Stanford University." Stanford, Calif., Stanford University Libraries, 1976, p.2. (pamphlet)

4. Blakely, Robert. "Projected Automated Systems Costs for: 1) Monographic Acquisitions, 2) Serials Acquisition, 3) Circulation and Inventory Control; FY66-FY77." Oct. 1965. (Unpublished report.)

5. FAUL Technical Services Committee. "FAUL/OCLC Feasibility Study" (A Report to Board Directors of the Five Associated University Libraries). Dec. 1971. (unpublished)

6. Cornell University Technical Services Department. "A Time/Cost Study of Processing Books Received via Unit Orders and Blanket Orders," *Five Associated University Libraries Newsletter* 3:4-9, July 1972.

7. Bayunus, Owais. *A Cost Analysis of the Automated Systems Control Group; The Acquisitions Department and the Catalog Department of the Central Technical Services; Cornell University Libraries.* Jan. 1975. (ED 102 996)

8. *Ibid.*

9. "Measuring How Office Workers Work," *Business Week*, Nov. 14, 1970, pp. 54-60.

10. Walker, Elaine. "OCLC in a University Library." Paper presented at Technical Services Coordinating Group, Joint Cataloguing Workshop of the Canadian Association of College and University Librarians, and the Canadian Library Association. Toronto, 1975. (Proceedings in process.)

11. *OCLC Newsletter* No. 75, Nov. 18, 1974, p.3.

12. Welch, Helen M. "Technical Service Costs, Statistics and Standards," *Library Resources & Technical Services* 11:436-42, Fall 1967.

A. ROBERT THORSON
Head, Circulation Department
The Ohio State University Libraries

The Economics of Automated Circulation

The title of this presentation is listed in the official program as "The Economics of Automated Circulation." A more accurate title might be "The Economics of Automated Circulation—the OSU Experience." The added subtitle is important because it is my intent to limit discussion to cost factors involved with the development and maintenance of LCS at The Ohio State University (OSU). LCS originally stood for Library Circulation System, but has subsequently come to mean Library Control System.

The purpose of this paper is not to justify the sizable monetary expenditures which were, and are, necessary to develop and maintain LCS, but rather to state as accurately as possible how much the system costs (both historically and currently), and to describe the benefits OSU library patrons and library administrators are receiving from the system.

This discussion, arranged according to historical development, includes: (1) the state of library service at OSU in the late 1960s, leading to the ultimate resolution to utilize automated techniques; (2) the service objectives of LCS and developmental costs; (3) ongoing operational costs; (4) the benefits derived from LCS; (5) plans for future systems development; and (6) a working example of possible circulation costs.

When Hugh Atkinson came to Ohio State in the spring of 1967, there was a somewhat ineffective automation committee, which seemed to spend most of its time examining current theories, reviewing the literature, and discussing promises of how automation could and would affect the future of library operations. By February 1968 the seven members of the automation committee were authorized to spend 10 percent of their time on the committee's activities.

From that time on, developments evolved rapidly, reflecting what was later stated by Jesse Shera:

> Let us for a moment, look at the computer, not for what it is, but a symbol of what is taking place in the library world, a harbinger of innovation, change, and the new era of the librarian's responsibility to society. The computer has...broken the hard crust of tradition and is forcing librarians for the first time to consider seriously the philosophical setting of their role in society.[1]

Concomitant to this, OSU became aware that it was necessary to explore new avenues in order to meet the diverse needs of the university community—a community of some 70,000 potential users, utilizing over twenty separate campus libraries holding more than 2 million volumes (a figure which has increased over the ensuing years to 3.5 million volumes).

Access to the collection, both in terms of circulation and cataloging practices, was often inadequate in the late 1960s. To cite a typical example, an OSU library user who knew what he or she wanted (that is, knowing author and/or title) had to go to the Main Library and consult the union catalog to determine whether the system owned that particular title and where, in the decentralized system, that title was located. The user would then go to the appropriate library and either locate the specific item, or discover that it was missing or charged out to another patron. In the latter case, the user had to return to the Main Library to determine whether other copies existed and their locations, and then go to other libraries until the item was found. Assuming that either a library employee or a patron found the item desired, the patron had to fill out a charge card indicating call number, volume and copy information, author and title, and adequate name and address information. For every physical item charged, a separate card was filled out.

Queuing at circulation desks was a serious problem, particularly in the Main Library where, until 1971, the stacks were closed to undergraduates. Closed stacks meant that students had to wait up to an hour either to receive their requested material, or to find out that such material was not on the shelf. Furthermore, in order to renew books, the user was required to return them to the library from which they had been borrowed.

Not only was this experience frustrating to the patron, but it was also frustrating to the circulation staff. In the Main Library, at least, it took much time to consult more than seventy trays of manual circulation cards, with many cards so poorly completed that they were unintelligible. Because most students assumed that at least one copy of every book listed in the union catalog was located in the Main Library, it was necessary to check the shelflist before paging materials. The statistics kept were misleading because of the complexity of the files and because overdue notices were sent out only sporadically.

In 1968, the British library scholar Richard Kimber said, "In a changing world, librarians have a responsibility not only to know about the ways in which libraries can use the techniques of automation, but also to be aware of the changes automation can bring to library service."[2] Why go to automation for answers? Alan Veaner answered this question in 1970.

> There are three major, practical reasons for undertaking the automation of library functions: (1) to do something less expensively, more accurately, or more rapidly, (2) *to do something which can no longer* be done effectively in the manual system because of increased complexity or overwhelming volume of operations, and (3) to perform some function which cannot now be performed in the manual system—providing always that the administrator actually wants to perform the new service, has the resources to pay for it, and is not endangering the performance of existing services for which there is an established demand.[3]

Although Ohio State had made basic decisions prior to and independent of Veaner's statement, the decisions made did fall within those guidelines. The first reason for undertaking automation, Veaner stated, was to do something less expensively, more accurately or more rapidly. To my knowledge the decision to automate circulation functions acknowledged the probability of increased expenditures, if not by the library, then by the university. It was expected that associated activities would be carried out more rapidly and with greater accuracy. Veaner's second reason, concerning the complexity and volume of operational files, with their implied threat of ultimate breakdown, has already been exemplified by the typical user's experience in retrieving materials. The third reason, to provide some function not now performed in a manual system, was an original objective of LCS.

From its inception, LCS was meant to involve more than keeping track of circulation records. It was also to provide a kind of remote catalog access capability, the files to be accessible by telephone during the hours the Main Library was open.

Before examining actual implementation costs of LCS, it is necessary to examine, briefly, its genesis. At the same time that the library system was exploring the techniques and uses of automation, the director of university budgets (also chairman of the university's Computer Coordinating Committee) was interested in certain requests made by the libraries for computer support. This interest prompted him to assign to the library a systems analyst charged with ascertaining what the library was actually doing and with helping channel its diverse efforts into a manageable program which might reasonably be carried out. This position evolved into the research and development (R&D) division of the university libraries, and personnel monies for that and one programming position were transferred to the library's personnel budget, effective November 1, 1968. The amount of transfer was $20,976.

Effective January 1, 1969, an additional $2,500 was allocated to support the R&D division's extensive analysis of library operations. The existing automation committee was disbanded and replaced by an automation implementation committee, whose membership was comprised of members of the highest levels of library management. It was this committee which ultimately determined that circulation should be the first library function to be automated. After being confirmed by the administrative staff conference, a proposal was presented to the budget director, who initially viewed it as "an enormously expensive system going up to do something that was already being done, even though poorly."[4] Over a period of several months, however, he became convinced of its advantages, particularly because it coincided with his current interest in restructuring the existing computing facilities at Ohio State University.

The time appeared to be right. The philosophical background had been set. The need for improved library service, particularly in circulation, was evident, and times were such that university administrators were willing to provide funds (funds more available then than now) for "innovative techniques."

IMPLEMENTATION COSTS

During 1969-70 there were three major related activities involved in the implementation of LCS: (1) the design of the system, (2) the selection and conversion of files, and (3) the arrangement for computing facilities and associated activities to maintain the system.

System Design

Because of the complexities involved and the fact that the libraries did not have the kind of expertise required to design on-line systems, the decision was made to employ an outside contractor. A detailed program of requirements was sent out on bid by the university. IBM was asked to submit a bid because of its previous experience with on-line systems, and as it happened, IBM was the only company to submit a bid. IBM offered their proposal on June 3, 1969, the title being "A Circulation System for The Ohio State University Libraries."

The bid was accepted and the contract let on July 8, 1969. It read: "Contract personnel services (i.e., IBM) for four people beginning September, 1969 to be billed monthly at rate of $23.50 an hr., not to exceed

9,576 hours. To be performed in conjunction with installation of a 360/50 computer system now on order, to design and program an on-line circulation system per IBM proposal dated June 3, 1969, entitled 'A Circulation System for The Ohio State University Libraries.' "

This contract committed the university to $225,036 for LCS development by IBM. One year later, on September 24, 1970, the libraries requested an additional 100 hours of programming to accomplish four tasks not originally outlined in the specifications. This cost was $2,350, making a total development cost of $227,386—this was the visible cost.

There were many hidden costs not included in this figure, as well as costs which cannot really be reconstructed or calculated. Literally thousands of hours of staff time were spent during this period responding to the detailed functional specifications as they were issued by IBM, re-educating and preparing themselves for what would surely be a traumatic experience, and training for the use of the system. Another hidden cost was computer testing time, a provision of the contract that required Ohio State University to provide that service. A memorandum dated August 25,1969 from the head of R&D to the automation implementation committee stated: "Arrangements for computer time at the computer center have been made for fiscal 1969/70 on a no-charge basis." Undoubtedly there were other internally absorbed costs, memories of which have been dimmed by the passage of time.

Selection and Conversion of Files

While IBM programmers were writing and testing programs, another important activity was going on—the conversion of the data base to a machine-readable format. Many months of consideration were spent in determining: (1) the file to be used for conversion, (2) the data elements to be converted, and (3) the vendor to do the actual conversion. This entire process has been adequately documented by Guthrie,[5] but the results need to be summarized here.

Conversion of the union catalog proved to be prohibitively expensive. The other major files available were the shelflist and the central serial record. Monetary considerations as well as accuracy and completeness of data led to the decision to convert a truncated version of the shelflist. The data elements selected for conversion were the Library of Congress classification number, author/main entry, title (not necessarily complete), edition statement when available, a holdings field containing volume and copy identification, and a location and circulation condition code which would identify and allow for multiple circulation periods for over twenty-five separate library locations. In order to provide additional information, other data elements were added to the original list: a non-English language indicator, the portfolio indicator, a size indicator (when necessary to determine oversize material) and, when available, the LC card number.

The decision to put the conversion out for bid was based primarily on the belief that "the University administration was more inclined to provide money for specific items with set dollar amounts than to allocate funds for personnel whose jobs might tend to continue past conversion time."[6] After analyzing the bidding procedures used by several other institutions and after developing detailed procedures and specifications for conversion, five potential vendors experienced in this kind of activity were invited to submit bids. Three responded, and as is typical with university fiscal authorities, the lowest bid—$87,900—was accepted.

The logistics being determined, the actual conversion began in late February 1970. Although completion was scheduled for June 19, 1970, the actual completion date was August 4. This did, however, fall within the testing dates required by IBM to fulfill its contractual obligations.

The number of records, or titles, converted was 736,051, comprising 64,931,814 characters. The final cost was $86,408.42, about $1,500 under the original estimated bid. The three principal costs were $1,500 for setup costs, $7,000 for the expense of additional edition statements, and $77,918.18 for keying at the rate of $1.20 per thousand characters. Because proofreading expenses were a responsibility of OSU, an additional amount of $8,126.40 must be added, bringing the total cost of the conversion project to $94,534.82, or an average cost of 12.8 cents per title converted.

The Arrangement for Computing Facilities

One aspect of the reorganization of computing facilities at Ohio State University was the formation of the Learning Resources Computer Center (LRCC), one of four centers broken apart from central facilities. LRCC was charged with providing support to three areas of the university: (1) testing and evaluation, (2) computer-assisted instruction, and (3) the library circulation system. It was this center, as stated in the contract with IBM, that had on order an IBM 360/50, as well as several dozen terminals. The center was given an initial operating budget of $500,000, plus a personnel budget of approximately $120,000. During LRCC's first year of operation, approximately 60 percent of its support went to LCS—about $372,000. This information more properly belongs with the discussion of ongoing costs, but does demonstrate the initial impetus given to the support of LCS.

Before LCS became operational, LRCC also paid the costs of establishing the telephone center. The charges for building the room, establishing stations, and installing carpeting and electrical circuits came to $6,010. LRCC also absorbed the initial costs charged by Ohio Bell Telephone for the establishment of network configurations necessary for LCS, including: (1) temporary service to LRCC, (2) lines for the IBM 2848, (3) lines for the IBM 2740's in the Main and departmental libraries, and (4) the installation of six operator work stations in the telephone center. The cost for lines and Ohio Bell equipment came to $2,760, not including projected monthly charges totaling $1,747.90. Of this figure, the telephone center costs came to $404.50, with projected monthly charges of $264.85.

It is not a simple task to summarize the implementation costs of LCS. Because of the complexity of activity going on during these formative years, it is difficult first, to distinguish accurately between implementation and ongoing costs; and second, to determine costs absorbed internally by the library system versus new allocation resources provided by the university. Atkinson did report in 1971 that the libraries never had a separate appropriation for library automation.[7] Although it appears that initial costs were paid from the general university budget, there is some evidence that the libraries did, in fact, provide at least $111,000 for the initial development. Table 1 is a tabulated summary of known and identifiable costs in implementing LCS.

ONGOING COSTS

Ongoing costs are subsumed in three principal categories: personnel costs, supplies, and computer support.

Personnel Costs

The only new positions funded because of automation were the telephone center operator positions. In the summer of 1970, $80,215 was transferred to the libraries' personnel budget to fund twenty-eight half-time positions. As of FY 1975/76 those same positions, minus one, cost $93,974.40—a 17 percent increase in six years. The increase was lower than might be expected, because of heavy turnover in that unit.

Although only two positions totaling $20,976 were transferred to the libraries, the R & D division's personnel budget over succeeding years must be considered, because its principal activities were in support of LCS (see Table 2). The principal reason for gradual decline over the years is that after another unit became responsible for file maintenance, the activities of that division diminished to the point that R & D no longer appears as a separate unit on the organization chart of the libraries. Responsibility for updating the files is now assigned to the automated file control unit. Its existence is first reflected in the personnel records for FY 1971/72. These positions were not separately funded, but resulted from internal reorganization within the libraries, particularly in technical services. Because their activities are associated exclusively with LCS, their ongoing budgets must also be examined (see Table 3). The automated file control unit, comprised of from three to five FTE personnel, prepared 77,184 records for optical scanning during 1974/75, and proofread 163,035 records passed through machine file maintenance that same year.

Programming contract—IBM	$225,036.00
additional programming	2,350.00
	$227,386.00
Shelflist conversion	$ 86,408.42
proofreading expenses	8,126.40
	$ 94,534.82
LRCC—one-time support	
telephone center construction	$ 6,010.00
telephone network configuration for system	2,760.00
	$ 8,770.00
R & D personnel costs (2 years)	
1968/69	$ 20,976.00
1969/70	$ 45,537.60
	$ 66,513.60
Grand Total	$397,204.42

Table 1. Known and Identifiable costs in Implementing LCS

1970/71	$61,164.80
1971/72	$33,865.00
1972/73	$36,232.80
1973/74	$15,648.00
1974/75	$16,248.00

Table 2. R&D Division's Personnel Budget

1971/72	$24,742.00
1972/73	$28,922.40
1973/74	$23,940.80
1974/75	$27,310.40
1975/76	$30,472.00

Table 3. Automated File Control Units Personnel Budget

The only personnel costs considered are those positions which would not have existed but for the development and continuation of LCS. Some argument could be made for including salaries of everyone presently involved in circulation activities, but the difficulties in prorating time devoted to circulation activities for persons performing a wide spectrum of functions negated this approach. Because these positions did exist under the manual system, and because a cost analysis of manual circulation functions at Ohio State University had never been made, it seemed prudent to avoid making an attempt to derive a total system circulation cost by title or, with lack of sound documentation, to conjure up a cost-benefit analysis that would not be meaningful or accurate. A hypothetical model will be described later in the presentation.

Supply Costs

The second large ongoing expense to the libraries is the cost of supplies and other miscellaneous costs. The monthly telephone bill for the telephone center is $312.00, the annual allocation from the libraries' operating budget being $3,745.00. In FY 1974/75, 275,000 patron notices (billings and overdues) were sent out. An order for 250,000 printer-runable cards comes to $1,342.50. Because more than one-half the number of patron notices mailed were to off-campus addresses, the postage alone came to a conservative $15,000. Obviously, the cost of the notices and postage vary with the frequency notices are generated and mailed.

The last major supply cost is for the thermal paper used in the printer terminals. Between May 16, 1974 and June 26, 1975, the libraries purchased 176 cases of thermal paper at a cost of $9,504.00. Although there is no separate budget for LCS supplies, a summary tabulation of the foregoing remarks may provide an approximate yearly ongoing supply cost (see Table 4).

Telephone statement	$ 3,745.00	
Patron notification cards	1,342.50	(approx.)
Terminal paper	9,504.00	(approx.)
Postage	15,000.00	(approx.)
Total	$29,591.50	

Table 4. Supply and Miscellaneous Costs

Computer Support

Ongoing computer support was initially provided by the Learning Resources Computer Center, which has since merged with other units to become the University Systems Computer Center (USCC). The first real evidence of cost factors appeared in an October 18, 1971, letter from J. Carroll Notestine to Hugh C. Atkinson:

> The following table lists the value of computer processing provided to your department during the past year by the Learning Resources Computer Center . . . .

October 1970	$11,710
November 1970	$31,510
December 1970	$32,320
January 1971	$32,910
February 1971	$27,940
March 1971	$31,390
April 1971	$26,810
May 1971	$30,570
June 1971	$23,170
July 1971	$28,250
August 1971	$24,070
September 1971	$21,070
TOTAL	$321,720

Specific costs were not identified. More explicit information was provided in a letter dated August 10, 1973, again from the director of USCC to the director of libraries. In this letter five functions of LCS are identified with their cost:

Hourly cost of operating LCS (computer only)	$48.50
Annual cost of one terminal	1,500.00
One maintenance (June 5, to be exact)	518.40
Overdues (June 17) - computer portion	56.30
- microfiche	274.40
Fine notices (June 25) - computer portion	182.10
- microfiche	224.00

The libraries currently receive on a monthly basis four detailed reports of services provided by USCC in support of LCS, the charges being billed to specific account numbers through the university's interdepartmental billing system. The four account statements are: (1) on-line production, (2) weekly update, (3) daily update, and (4) support tasks. February 1976 statements will serve to illustrate.

On-line production costs or charges are divided into three categories: (1) computer services, (2) data preparation, and (3) fixed cost services. The total cost of services provided and charged to this account was $35,363.70. Computer services represented 78 percent of the total charges, or $27,537.90, of which core time accounted for $22,778.54 and CPU time for $4,676.39. Data preparation, or optical character recognition processing, that month was $225 or less than one percent of the total charges. Fixed cost services came to $7,600.80, or 21 percent of the total charges to this account. Of this figure, $6,415.80 was for terminal, line, and port costs. Three other terminal costs ($450) were itemized separately because funds for them had been permanently transferred from the libraries to the center. Also included were delivery service from the research center—$25; clerical support—$372; COM—$225; and the purchase of ten magnetic tapes—$100.

The weekly update account for February listed $2,250.45 for computer services, $105.00 for data preparation, and a $33.40 adjustment for errors. CPU time amounted to $1,272.35, and core time cost $826.12. Because 248,382 lines were printed, output charges were $151.44. This account basically represents the LCS and OCLC batch maintenance runs.

The daily update account for February listed computer services at a cost of $840.61: $398.66 for CPU time, $214.60 for core time, and $232.63 for lines printed. This account basically represents the printing of daily notices and daily fine maintenance.

The last account—support tasks—listed $376.09 in service, $84.80 for CPU time, $175.70 for core time, $102.90 for lines printed, and $12.69 for report processing. This account represents mainly overdue notices and billings.

The total of these four accounts for February 1976 came to $38,902.45. Costs vary from month to month, but over the years the principal increase has been in the on-line production support because of increased use of CPU time and core time. The cost of the charge unit has not changed since January 1972, but many changes have been effected in order to improve LCS. Veaner was correct in saying: "Although unit machine costs are going down all the time, the more one has of a cheap resource...the more one is likely to use it, and the net effect may be more money spent....Consequently, the more facilities automation gives us, the more likely are we to need more resources rather than less."[8]

The director of USCC estimates the support value given to LCS at $410,000 per year, exclusive of programming time. Currently there is the equivalent of three full-time programmers assigned to library tasks at an annual cost estimated at $60,000. Although a part of USCC's budget, the libraries permanently transferred $8,568 to USCC in January 1973 for programming. Assuming the figure of $410,000 to be correct, the average monthly charge (or more accurately, support value) is $34,166.66, or approximately $4,735 less than February's statement.

Two summary tabulations are provided to illustrate ongoing computer service costs per year. Figures given are based on two assumptions: (1) $410,000 represents a reasonable estimate of total ongoing computer services costs; and (2) the February 1976 statements are representative, and can therefore be used to project annual cost percentages for both the four accounting activities and the basic computer services. Table 5 represents costs by account and Table 6 represents costs by activity.

A further analysis is necessary to determine percentages of computer support ($326,565.00) which can be attributed to CPU time, core space, and output:

Central processing unit costs	$ 68,578.65	21%
Core space	251,455.05	77%
Output	6,531.30	2%
	$326,565.00	100%

A final summary of current ongoing LCS costs, given the foregoing parameters, may be tabulated as follows:

Personnel costs, solely identified with LCS as of September 1975		
Telephone Center	$93,974.40	
AFC	30,472.00	
		$124,446.40
Supplies		
Telephone center lines	$ 3,745.00	
Patron notification cards	1,342.50	
Terminal paper	9,504.00	
Postage	15,000.00	
		$ 29,591.50
Computer support		
Hardware	$410.000.00	
Software	60,000.00	
		$470,000.00 EST
		$624,037.90

Activity	*Subcost*	*% of Activity Total*	*Activity Total*	*% of Total*
On-line Processing			$373,100.00	91
computer support	$291,018.00	78		
fixed costs	78,351.00	21		
data preparation	3,731.00	1		
	$373,100.00	100		
Weekly Update			$ 24,600.00	6
computer support	23,376.00	95		
data preparation	1,230.00	5		
	$24,600.00	100		
Daily Update			$ 8,200.00	2
computer support	8,200.00	100		
Support Tasks			$ 4,100.00	1
computer support	3,977.00	97		
report processing	123.00	3		
	4,100.00	100		
Total			$410,000.00	100

Table 5. Costs by Account Statement

Considering the monies spent on the development of LCS and the extensive support needed to maintain and improve the system, the casual (or not so casual) observer may well question the results. The benefits derived can be grouped into two categories: (1) improved service to library users, and (2) benefits provided to library managers.

From its inception, LCS was designed to provide improved services to library users. It was known that costs would exceed those incurred under a manual system but, given the climate prevalent in the late 1960s, the automation of circulation functions appeared to be inevitable. A typical library user situation was described early in this paper. In contrast, the following situation now prevails. The library user, who knows what he or she wants, calls an operator at a central telephone number (whenever the Main Library is open) who acts as liaison between patron and the computer records. The operator can tell the patron whether the library system has the particular book in question. If the system does not have the title, the operator can ascertain if the title has been ordered and, if received, where it is located in the stream of technical processing, in which case a "patron save" can be placed, and the processing expedited.

Activity	*Subcost*	*% of Activity Total*	*Total*	*% of Total*
Computer support			$326,565.00	79.65
accounts 1	$291,018.00	89		
2	23,370.00	7		
3	8,200.00	3		
4	3,977.00	1		
	$326,565.00	100		
Data Preparation		100	4,961.00	1.00
Fixed Costs			78,351.00	1.90
Terminals	$70,750.95	90.3		
COM	3,839.20	4.9		
Clerical support	2,663.93	3.4		
Other	1,096.92	1.4		
	$78,351.00	100		
Report processing			123.00	6.00
			$410,000.00	

Table 6. Costs by Activity

After determining that the library has a particular book, the operator can tell the patron which departmental libraries have copies available for circulation. LCS does not at present indicate individual volume holdings of serials, but the operator can inform the patron which volumes and copies are currently charged out. If the request is for a monograph, and if a copy is available, the operator can perform the charge transaction immediately. After verifying the patron's address in the computer files, the operator, if the address is on campus, offers the patron the option of picking the book up or having it sent through the campus mail delivery service. If the operator tells the patron that an item is not owned or not available, it does save the patron's valuable time which would be wasted in running from location to location.

Because most book collections on campus are open to the public, the patron, if he or she has found what was desired, need only bring materials to the circulation desk and provide legitimate identification. Rather than requiring the patron to fill out charge cards for each item, the terminal operator keys in the appropriate information. Renewals can be made by telephone or by mail, a sharp contrast to previous circulation procedures.

The following list summarizes the basic services provided library users because of LCS—services unique to the system, and services formerly provided so seldom or sporadically as to be totally ineffective.

1. Only one file need be consulted in order to determine the location and holdings of monographs, as well as the availability of both serials and monographs.
2. The user need not consult the union catalog in the Main Library in order to find out where a book is located. This search access to the files, as well as the charging of materials, may be performed by telephoning a central access number or by visiting any circulation unit housing a terminal. When appropriate, books will be mailed.
3. The user receives, on a regular basis, overdue (fines-billing), recall, and book-available (or not available) notices, thus eliminating many frustrations caused by the lack of adequate communication which existed under the manual system.
4. Unless other patrons have requested circulating materials, renewals can be accomplished by telephone or by mail.
5. A book which is unavailable because it is presently in circulation can be recalled by placing a save transaction on the title. This automatically reduces the loan period of the person having the book, and allows a seven-day grace period for return before a fine is incurred. When the book is discharged, it is automatically charged to the first requestor and (if so opted) mailed.
6. Bibliographies, checklists, etc., will be checked against the libraries' holdings file upon request.
7. Uncataloged items (i.e. cataloging arrearage) are entered in LCS with a "dummy call number," and can circulate normally through the system.
8. A book recently ordered or in the process of being cataloged can now be accessed from any terminal and a save may be placed against that title (that is, when the book becomes available, it will be charged automatically to the requestor and, if so desired, sent through campus mail).
9. Some unique collections not represented in the card catalog are more conveniently accessible than ever before. These include, in addition to the cataloging backlog, the Human Area Relations Files, the ERIC documents (in microform), the juvenile collection, and the musical score collection, among others.

This represents a simplistic view of LCS patron services, yet encompasses the essence of the system's philosphy. Not only does the library user benefit, but a number of computer-generated reports provide library managers with tools which aid in the analysis of existing operations and, it is hoped, will provide a basis for decision-making for the future. These reports include:

1. A daily notification of requested books which were not physically located at the time the request was made. Such information allows circulation

personnel to concentrate efforts on "tracking down" these elusive materials.

2. A daily notification of items charged or discharged using the error option; in other words, items which could be charged utilizing LCS, but which necessitated overriding normal procedures in order to accomplish the transaction. This feature brings to attention cases of noncompliance with established practices and allows for the reinstatement of previously withdrawn titles and the correction of materials incorrectly entered in the system.
3. A daily listing of titles so much in demand that three or more patrons have officially requested each of them. This report is used to determine the advisability of acquiring additional copies.
4. A daily listing of books reported lost by patrons. Again this represents a tool for the acquisition of replacements.

These reports have been made available since the inception of LCS. The following reports have resulted from requests made after IBM turned LCS over to the university:

1. A quarterly listing of books which are so long overdue (at least twenty weeks) that the system assumes they are lost; the patron charged with said items is billed accordingly.
2. COM copies of overdues, billings and student address information, which allows the telephone center operator and/or the Library Budget Office to respond rapidly to patron requests.
3. "Snap-shots" of the circulation-save file, and/or master file, provided upon request.
4. Monthly circulation statistics, organized first by function (charge, discharge, renewal, saves and snags), and further subdivided by library location and patron class.
5. Monthly statistics, by terminal, of all transactions processed—a valuable tool in determining new locations or possible relocations of terminals.

The plans for the future of LCS automated library activities were thoroughly described by Robert Daugherty in a paper given at the Midwest Academic Librarians Conference in 1975.[9] The two most important activities are: (1) the inclusion of serial holdings in the masterfile, and (2) on-line maintenance of the master file. Accomplishing the first goal would allow the remote circulation of serials, something which cannot be done at present and will provide, when appropriate, both a summary statement of holdings and a listing of serial holdings by physical unit. Programming for this is well under way and, as of this presentation, testing is in progress.

In terms of long-range progress, on-line maintenance of the LCS master record is next in priority. This would eliminate the present weekly updates and allow temporary additions of test files, photocopies, reprints, etc., to the master file; with on-line maintenance capabilities, the library can add to the file whatever it wishes and, or course, assume the responsibilities.

This brief summary of major future programs for LCS, as well as plans for completely providing information access to all materials owned and housed by OSU libraries, suggests a total minisystems concept of future developments.

It has been stated several times, and for various reasons, that it was not a purpose of this study either to present a cost-benefit analysis of LCS, or to provide a definitive circulation-unit cost. It does seem appropriate, however, to address the question briefly, particularly because it is a question of general interest. The only cost study of LCS was that done by Guthrie in 1972. In a memorandum dated February 16, 1972 from Guthrie to Atkinson, Guthrie reported that, within the limitations of his investigation, the unit cost per circulation was $0.39, not including labor or supply costs. The figure generally quoted for the cost of circulating a book through LCS is $0.44. This figure was based primarily on department library statistics, and although it included labor costs, it also included manual reserve circulation. The complexity of library operations and the lack of systematic and detailed job cost analysis negate any attempt to reconstruct this study or to bring it up to date.

It seems, rather, more appropriate (or perhaps more cowardly) to examine one unit and the costs associated with its operation, and derive an approximate unit cost figure which might be useful, although meaningful only in terms of the operations of that unit.

The telephone center is a unique unit of the library system—a unit whose job functions are exclusively devoted to LCS in general, and to circulation functions in particular. The number and type of transactions performed in that unit can be monitored monthly by means of LCS statistical reports, although Ohio Bell has never provided any statistics relative to the number of calls received in a given time period.

Personnel costs are available and, given the assumption that the six terminals in the center represent 10 percent of the ongoing computer costs (exclusive of software), certain figures can easily be derived.

The ongoing costs in Table 6 are attributable to the telephone center's operation, based primarily on 1974/75 figures. Supplies other than telephone billings are discounted, for this unit (at least theoretically) has only CRTs and is not a library unit in which books are located.

Excluding the 58,000 changes made to the name and address file during 1974/75, the terminals in the center recorded 728,197 valid transactions. For this unit, the average cost per transaction was $0.185, regardless of type of transaction. If only charges and renewals are used, the transactions number 218,551, resulting in a unit cost of $0.62. A circulation transaction does,

LCS ongoing costs (10%)	$ 41,000.00
Personnel	89,684.00
Telephone billing	3,744.00
Air conditioning (rental unit)	350.00
TOTAL	$134,778.00

Table 6. Telephone Center Costs

however, involve more than the initial charge, and possible subsequent renewals. For every charge transaction there must be a corresponding discharge transaction. In this sphere of activity, the telephone center is definitely atypical, for its discharge function is limited to Main Library books, and the vast majority of Main Library books are not discharged by that unit.

In 1974/75, the center did perform 239,834 transactions directly associated with circulation (i.e. charge, renewal, and discharge transactions). By adding the discharge transaction, the unit cost decreases from $0.62 to $0.56 per LCS circulation transaction, not including the physical retrieval of materials, nor their subsequent reshelving.

Due to the fact that LCS is also a remote catalog access system, the computer file searching statistics must also be considered. During 1974/75, the telephone center performed 2,777 author searches (a search capability implemented in March 1975), 8,276 shelflist searches, 118,655 general searches, and 217,574 detailed searches. Therefore, the number of transactions devoted to the catalog access capability of LCS was 347,282, or approximately $0.385 per transaction. During 1974/75, the department terminals registered a total of 1,921,657 transactions, which can conveniently be divided into two kinds of activity—catalog access function transactions and circulation activity functions—as follows:

Catalog Access Transactions		*Circulation Activity Transactions*		
AUS	5,952	Charges		239,324
SPS	19,331	Renewals		213,542
General searches	594,626	subtotal	452,866	
Detailed searches	607,036	Discharges		219,805
Total	1,226,945	subtotal	672,671	
		Snags		4,395
		Saves		17,646
			Total	694,712

The easiest way to determine the cost of an individual transaction is to divide monies expended by the number of terminal transactions. Depending on the figures used, a number of permutations are possible. For this quasi-intellectual exercise the following two tabulations are offered.

A. Terminal command transaction unit costs, based only on personnel and the cost of supplies. The amount is $258,000 and represents the major LCS costs currently included in the libraries' budget:

1.	Cost per transaction	$00.13
2.	Cost per catalog access transaction	$00.21
3.	Cost per circulation activity transaction	$00.37
4.	Cost per circulation (charges and renewals)	$00.57
5.	Cost per circulation (charges, renewals and discharges)	$00.38

B. Transaction unit costs based on the above with the addition of the calculated support ($360,500) provided by USCC:

1.	Cost per transaction	$00.19
2.	Cost per catalog access transaction	$00.29
3.	Cost per circulation activity transaction	$00.52
4.	Cost per circulation (charges and renewals)	$00.80
5.	Cost per circulation (charges, renewals, and discharges)	$00.54

These contrived cost units do not include any manual charges, nor do they take into account any multiple transactions performed. For example, one charge command may result in the circulation of five books. Although the number of multiple transactions is not known, it is probably not a significant figure.

So far I have discussed only terminal command transactions. There are also file maintenance transactions, daily notifications, overdues, billings, etc. Consequently, the 3,947,814 terminal command transactions do not reflect a complete picture of LCS. Further study needs to be made before attempting to determine unit costs for other kinds of transactions, or for other library units.

Perhaps the most significant figure I can leave with you is a systems-only cost per circulation. In 1974/75, a total of 907,760 items were charged or renewed through LCS. Total ongoing costs have been identified at $624,038. The unit cost for circulation is $0.685.

There is, I believe, a statement in the *Talmud* which states that if one wants to understand the invisible, he must look closely at the visible. In terms of library automation costs, the reverse is true: if one wants to understand the visible, he must look carefully at the invisible.

REFERENCES

1. Shera, Jessie H. "The Quiet Stir of Thought, or, What the Computer Cannot Do," *Library Journal* 94:2879-80, Sept. 1, 1969.

2. Kimber, Richard T. *Automation in Libraries*. Oxford, England, Pergamon Press, 1968, p. 1.

3. Veaner, Allen. "Major Decision Points in Library Automation," *College & Research Libraries* 31:303-04, Sept. 1970.

4. Atkinson, Hugh C. "The Evolution of an Automated Circulation System." In *An Automated On-line Circulation System: Evaluation, Development, Use*. Columbus, Ohio, The Ohio State University Libraries, Office of Educational Services, 1973, p 4.

5. Guthrie, Gerry D. "Conversion of the Shelf List to Machine Readable Format." In *An Automated On-line Circulation System..., op.cit.*

6. *Ibid.*, p. 14.

7. Atkinson, *op cit.,* p.6.

8. Veaner, *op. cit.*, p. 307.

9. Daugherty, Robert A. "The Future and On-Line Control." Paper presented at the 20th Annual Meeting, Midwest Academic Librarians Conference, Columbus, Ohio, May 23, 1975. (unpublished)

MARTHA WEST
Associate Professor
Department of Librarianship
San Jose State University
San Jose, California
and
BRETT BUTLER
Director
Butler Associates

Performance Measures in Automated Systems Management

When first approached as a possible speaker on the subject of performance benefit measures for library automation, my immediate reaction was that there are no such measures. Considerable cogitation, consultation, and survey of the literature hasn't made me change my mind, but my coauthor has convinced me that there is a beginning to the development of such measures in the actual management of automated systems today. This, then, is the thrust of our paper.

The reality of the situation in most American libraries today is that automated services are neither so well established nor so stable that normal professional management methods suffice for control and evaluation of the application. That is, the cost accounting and budget reporting which are standard in most business (and some public agency) environments are not suited to the management of rapidly changing operations. By normal standards of library operations, most automated services are characterized by a rate of change—of procedures, methods, services delivered, and costs—which can only be described as radical in the organizational sense.

Based on the limitation of the title of this paper, we are therefore limiting the consideration of these management techniques to the citation of some relevant works in the bibliography. In this paper, we consider the management techniques related to what has become widely know as "program management"—the techniques of most direct relevance.

Having defined our scope by fiat as program management, it is useful to identify briefly what generally available techniques are used outside the information community to control programs. Table 1 highlights the features of seven management program evaluation techniques. Swanson has done an excellent job reducing the intellectual content of these techniques to a set of comparable abbreviated statements.[1] The most striking result is the interchangeability of most steps of most of the techniques described.

The rather scanty literature on performance evaluation in libraries can be classified into three groups. The *global* tries to measure performance related in some way to user satisfaction or societal goals. The *supervisory* discusses specific techniques for measuring productivity or effort in very specific environments, such as the relative value of various copiers for catalog card reproduction. Automated library systems in general do not fit well into either group noted above. Rather, they may be considered as projects which can be subjected to *strategic* evaluation. In other words, the automated system per se is designed to fit some broader set of policy goals; it is not reasonable to fault it for not delivering a service outside its design scope. For example, a management goal in an academic library may be: (1) to provide catalog access more effectively at the location of the present card catalog, or (2) to provide catalog access on a distributed basis all over the campus. The automated system selected can reasonably be evaluated only within the scope of the specific goal selected.

It is, of course, true that many automated systems are designed and built without such explicit identification of policy goals, but the shortcomings in the resultant operation are not failures in the performance of the automated system.

From a practical point of view, the choice of a specific evaluation technique within the library should depend primarily on evaluation of which technique is presently held in best repute by the library's parent organization. The actual use of any of these systematized guidelines, or any management-based logical alternative, will result in the provision of sufficient information for program management—if the technique is well and thoughtfully applied. None of these general techniques will substitute for intelligent thought about the library's specific needs and problems.

We are making an initial primary assertion regarding the management of automated library services: for most libraries, the automated services which are going to be used over the next few years will change with enough rapidity that each application should be considered as a specific program rather than a

System Analysis (SA)[74]	*Operations Research (OR)*[1]	*Benefit-Cost Analysis (BCA)*[142,207]
1. Examine and clarify objectives; define issues of concern and problems	1. Find the problem to be solved (decision to be made)	1. Estimate the demand for proposed goods or services
2. Determine alternative courses of action that have some chance of resolving the issues	2. Determine the objectives to be accomplished (outcomes desired)	2. Determine alternative production possibilities
3. Establish good criteria for choosing among the alternatives	3. Identify the alternative courses of action available nd the possible outcomes of each alternative	3. Identify legal, resource, and technical constraints on the choice of alternatives
4. Obtain data (quantitative where possible) on the economic costs, effectiveness or benefits, and risks of the alternatives	4. Derive a measure of performance for evaluating the alternatives with respect to the probabilities of achieving the desired objectives	4. Select a benefit-cost criterion measure for choosing among the alternatives
5. Construct models capable of predicting the consequences that are likely to follow from each choice of alternatives	5. Obtain information on controllable variables and on aspects of the environment (noncontrollable variables) that can affect the outcomes of the alternatives	5. Obtain information on the resource requirements, expected revenues, other direct benefits, possible side effects, intangibles, and uncertainties for each feasible alternative
6. Compare results of applying the model to the alternatives in terms of the consequences	6. Construct a model that yields the performance measure as a function of the relationship among the variables	6. Compare and rank the alternatives on their benefit/cost ratios
7. Using predictions obtained from the models and other relevant information needed for further comparison of the alternatives, derive conclusions and recommend a course of action	7. Obtain solutions of the model, i.e., find values of the controllable variables that produce the best performance for specified values of the uncontrolled variables	7. Include information on intangible (unpriced) and unmeasurable (not quantifiable) gain and loss factor not incorporated in benefit cost computations for each alternative
8. Test the conclusions wherever possible	8. Select and implement the test solution	
	9. Test the implementation; modify as necessary	

[74]FISHER, GENE H. Cost Considerations in Systems Analysis. American Elsevier Publishing Co., Inc. New York, N.Y., 1971, 325 pp.

[1]ACKOFF, RUSSELL L.; SASIENI, MAURICE W. Fundamentals of Operations Research. John Wiley & Sons, Inc., New York, N.Y., 1968, 451 pp.

[142]MCKEAN, ROLAND N. Efficiency in Government Through Systems Analysis with Emphasis on Water Resources Development. A Rand Corporation Research Study. John Wiley & Sons, Inc., New York, N.Y., 1958. 336 pp.

[207]SEWELL, W. R. D.; DAVIS, J.; SCOTT, A. D.; ROSS, D. W. Guide to Benefit-Cost Analysis. Queen's Printer and Controller of Stationery, Ottawa, Canada, 1965. 49 pp.

[238]U.S. CONGRESS, SENATE COMMITTEE ON GOVERNMENT OPERATIONS, SUBCOMMITTEE ON NATIONAL SECURITY AND INTERNATIONAL OPERATIONS. Planning-Programming-Budgeting; Budget Bureau Guidelines of 1968, 90th Congress, 2d Session, Government Printing Office, Washington, D.C., 1968, 19 pp.

[92]HELLER, EDWARD D. Value Management: Value Engineering and Cost Reduction. Addison-Wesley Publishing Co., Reading, Mass., 1971, 229 pp.

[9]APPLEY, LAWRENCE A. "Standards of Management Performance." In: Business Policy, A Management Audit Approach. Edited by William T. Greenwood. Macmillan Co., New York, N.Y., 1967, 55-58.

Table 1. Evaluation Techniques

Planning-Programming-Budgeting (PPB)[238]	*Value Analysis/Engineering (VA/E)*[92]	*Management Audit (MA)*[9,136]	*Evaluation (EVAL)*[218,221,259]
1. Identify Major Program Issues (MPI's) (questions requiring budget decisions) 2. Produce program structures that show (1) program categories disclosing major objectives or scales of operation, (2) program subcategories or groupings of program elements according to output similarities, and (3) program elements or activities that yield a discrete output or end-product or related outputs 3. Derive measurable program objectives; determine alternative programs to meet the objectives; collect data and perform analyses to compare and assess the costs, sources of funds, and anticipated benefits of each alternative 4. Present decisions on choices in Program Memoranda (PM's) that summarize the analytic bases for the choices 5. Produce a Program and Financial Plan (PFP) that relates data on outputs, costs, and financing sources for each program by program element for the past, current, and budget years and four future years	1. Obtain information on customer needs, specifications and preferences about products and/or services 2. Obtain information on resource (input), production, and distribution costs 3. Establish, compare and assess alternatives 4. Reach a decision 5. Plan, develop, and implement the alternative(s) decided upon 6. Assess implementation; modify if necessary	1. Obtain information on company policies, organization, operating methods, financial procedures, personnel practices, and physical facilities 2. Obtain information on company's investors, suppliers, customers, and competitors and on company's industry 3. Identify problems and policy issues; prioritize them from major to minor; obtain facts and reasons for their existence 4. Analyze and appraise company's condition and industry position 5. Establish, compare, and assess alternative solutions to problems and issues 6. Prepare recommendations for revisions or change	1. Identify system to be studied, its elements their characteristics, and purposes of evaluation 2. Specify criteria, criterion variables and decision rules; state assumptions on which these will be based 3. Obtain information on system variables (input, output, transactional, and intervening variables that may influence system operations and performance) and on the antecedent system if applicable and possible 4. Compare outcomes with criteria on the decision rules, draw conclusions, make recommendations 5. Assemble analyzed data in a format appropriate for decision-makers; disseminate report 6. Design and assess alternatives to produce needed modifications or changes 7. Reach a decision 8. Plan, develop, and implement alternative(s) decided upon 9. Assess implementation; modify if necessary

[136]MARTINDELL, JACKSON. "The Management Audit." In Business Policy, A Management Audit Approach. Edited by William T. Greenwood, Macmillan Co., New York, N.Y. 1967, 83-91.

[218]STAKE, ROBERT E. "The Countenance of Educational Evaluation." Teachers College Record, 68:7 (April 1967) 523-540.

[221]STUFFLEBEAM, DANIEL L.; FOLEY, WALTER J.; GEPHART, WILLIAM J.; GUBA, EGON G.; HAMMOND, ROBERT L.; MERRIMAN, HOWARD O.; PROVUS, MALCOLM M. Educational Evaluation and Decision Making. F.E. Peacock Publishers, Inc., Itasca, Ill., 1971, 367 pp.

[259]WEISS, CAROL H. Evaluation Research, Methods for Assessing Program Effectiveness. Prentice-Hall, Inc., Englewood Cliffs, N.J., 1972, 160 pp.

Table 1. Evaluation Techniques

Source: Swanson, Rowena W. "Design and Evaluation of Information Systems." *Annual Review of Information Science and Technology* 10:54-55, 1975.

permanent service or fixture of the library's operation. For example, we would apply normal cost analysis techniques to the measure of performance in card filing if we assumed the card catalog would be a fixture of the specific library under study. If we assume implementation of any alternative to the card catalog, however, we can expect to see the use of several automated services over the coming decade. In a recent interview with public librarians who had been managing a book-catalog system for several years, we were discussing acceptance of the newly installed microform catalog. One person commented: "The patrons used to ask for the card catalog; now they ask where the book catalog went." The card catalog had lasted a century; the book catalog disappeared after a decade. There is no indication in the technology that this library (or any other) should expect a diminishing rate of change.

If this assertion is valid, and if the presentations by the other speakers confirm the growing feasibility of expanding the library's use of automated services, then the management of benefit analysis becomes a program management function.

While the jargon of professional business management is at least as confusing as the language of librarianship, the English-language definition of *program* delineates our intent sufficiently (in fact, the three disparate elements illustrate facets of the topic): (1) a prospectus or syllabus, (2) the events or pieces...of an entertainment or ceremony, and (3) a plan of procedure. There is one aspect common to these three definitions: a program is finite but not (except in the past tense) completed. A program is a project or an undertaking rather than a function. Collection development is a function of the library; a review of the holdings in a specific field against a standard list is a project.

Neither the history of automated library programs, nor the projections of likely changes in automated services, suggest that these programs can become functions. Change will occur rapidly enough so that a specific automated project can expect to have a lifespan of no more than a few years.

There are a number of program management and evaluation techniques which are widely used (or at least discussed) within the data processing industry, where rapid and continual change is accepted as normal. As with general management tools, we are excluding review of these techniques here on three related grounds:

1. Only a very few library systems have or will have the responsibility (or luxury) of selecting and controlling the computer operations environment within which they will operate. It does little good to know a great deal about structured programming management, if you buy your services from a book catalog vendor or OCLC.

2. Program management techniques rarely provide specific methods appropriate to library applications per se particularly because library applications tend to be more complex in terms of textual and language processing requirements than typical data processing jobs.
3. In our opinion, technicians both inside and outside the library community have overstated the importance to library administrators of knowing the relative efficiency of various computer equipment and software elements.

The key elements in program management of automated library applications are, rather, involved with how the library management defines its goals in specifying a new (automated) service, and then measures the results. This process is performance measurement. The term *performance measurement* necessarily implies the management of the program: else why bother taking the measure?

We are really, then, only interested in two elements. We want to measure the potential of the automation product to be procured, to define its potential task in the organization, and to define its costs. We then want to measure the results, in two major ways: (1) the degree to which the product delivered meets the specification; and (2) the way in which the product meets the target goals.*

Between goals and specifications lies a tricky gray area: one must communicate the initial design concept to others. This may involve communicating a technical systems concept up the organization chart to management or horizontally to other staff. It may involve explaining a management concept—balancing collection to measured user demand—to several different staff groups. In the areas of interest here, it almost certainly will involve communicating to "vendors," whether private contractors or one's own agency data processing operation.

In fact, it is probably the difficulties of keeping track of events through this gray area that accounts for the fact that so few projects report both prior planning and subsequent evaluations. We have a lot of literature discussing project plans, and there is a substantial amount of analysis of existing services. Whenever one organization has lived through the real implementation of an abstract plan, groping through the gray areas (where the fine black-and-white plans dissolve or at least become confused) seems to sap the organization's energies below the level required to complete the follow-up performance evaluation.

This observation does not particularly suggest that implementing an automated system is generally such a traumatic and unsuccessful experience that nobody wants to talk about it afterward. It seems more to be the result of

*It is not necessary for a product to meet specifications in order to meet performance goals; and conversely, a product built exactly to specification may fail to meet the organization's goals.

two factors: (1) as noted above, automated library systems are projects; new projects arrive and absorb the time which otherwise might be allocated to evaluating the old; and (2) few automation projects specifically include the formal evaluation phase in the project development plan.

Program Development

Evaluation and measurement of targets and results is probably more important during implementation than during planning or after operations are established. It is not difficult to envision a number of ways in which automated services can improve library operations, although the selection of the specific alternative can present an extremely difficult decision. In addition, the evaluation of results in the broader sense is limited by the ability of the library to implement parallel experimental designs, so operating evaluations are primarily useful for management purposes or for defining a new project.

If the proper evaluation of results being obtained during implementation is not made, however, one can experience failures in performance ranging from the catastrophic (never reaching the operating stage) to the merely annoying ("Why didn't we remember to include that data in the conversion?").

It is axiomatic that before a program can be evaluated it must be defined and understood. An automated library system must be defined both in terms of present operations and desired goals. It is nonetheless necessary to present this axiom because there are so many illustrations of automated applications where only a portion of the goals are explicitly identified and where, therefore, full evaluation cannot be made. While other papers at this clinic illustrate quite clearly the processes used to quantify the goal of "saving money," too often the other major goal of a system project is expressed at the level of "increased services," which is difficult, if not impossible, to measure.

For instance, in implementing a cataloging system, does the service goal relate to increasing the convenience of use for the cataloging department, for the public, or for some combination? To answer this type of question, it is necessary to define each program component into discrete units which can be compared in a manual vs. automated mode with regard to: (1) old functions partially or totally discontinued, (2) new functions established, (3) functions with little or no change, and (4) revised procedures within a function. For each of these, it is necessary to identify the overhead or fixed portions of the functions, so the analysis can be quite clear with regard to which functions are potentially variable. Otherwise we fall into the fallacy of what Allen Veaner has termed the "anyhow" school of economics, illustrated by the classic phrase, "But we have the computer anyhow, so it won't cost us anything to...."

Fundamental to this analysis is the identification, formulation, and communication to organization members of program goals as related to the present system and as projected. These goals also need to be related to the parent organization's goals. It is essential to make clear whether the automated system is merely changing procedural or administrative processes by which present goals are being met, or whether the system is implementing new goals. One indication is that planning described almost entirely in terms of relative costs generally implies continuation of present goals, with the major change in the automated system seen as cost control.

Early automated systems almost entirely represented continuation of general library organization goals. This is illustrated by early efforts to automate library catalogs primarily to eliminate filing costs. Current efforts are much more involved in fulfilling expanded service goals such as the effort to automate library catalogs in order to decentralize access. Because the automated system in the current environment cannot be compared directly to the old manual processes (the automated orange is different than the manual apple), it is particularly important to specify the degree and manner in which it is expected the library operation will change. This cannot be done after development and implementation have occurred.

It is likely that some of the desired goals will be extremely difficult to quantify. There are basically three areas to consider during program development: (1) the "hard" evaluation data available or obtainable, (2) the "soft" evaluation information, and (3) the definition of the local environment (technical and political). As available information is "hard" and "soft," so some performance measures will be "hard" or "soft," depending on the level of management confidence in the information obtained. But consideration of these three areas during program development will at least provide a framework for management.

Various definitions of management focus on an identification of the key management role as "decision-making in the presence of insufficient information," or a variation of the phrase. So it is the recognition of the range in which "hard" information becomes "soft" for evaluation purposes that is important. The effort to gain perfect information in order to make a perfect decision results in no decision being made at all.

Hard Evaluation Data

In general, costs are thought of as "hard" data; the mere presence of numeric data implies quantification (to an often unwarranted degree). It is the basic cost information which is being increasingly reviewed by the library's "controllers" (boards of trustees, regents, county supervisors, or legislators) who are experiencing increased problems in stretching the various taxpayers' dollars. It is, for instance, unlikely that we will see many automated library systems implemented in the next decade which baldly admit to an increased level of cost. At the very least, the most sophisticated descriptions now stress reduction in the rate of cost increase, or in the per-unit cost of operation. The latter formulation, first promulgated regularly during the development of the BALLOTS system, is also cited by OCLC and (with supporting real operating figures) by the Ohio State University circulation system.

In cost analysis, it is unfortunately necessary to know what our existing costs are, a process much less glamorous than budgeting new future programs. While a number of methodologies exist for determining costs (and the choice of which to use will lie within the expertise and constraints of the particular institution), a warning must be given. Because of the total absence of standardized task definitions within library operations (Have we been able to reach a consensus on what constitutes original cataloging?) the local costs obtained are only going to be applicable to the particular institution collecting them. They cannot be compared exactly to the costs calculated at similar institutions and, indeed, probably cannot even be validated to proper experimental standards.

The goal for most libraries, however, is to establish the level or magnitude of costs to be compared. It is not reasonable to concern the evaluation effort with determination of current costs to the penny or 1 percent level of accuracy for two reasons. First, the comparative costs of the projected automated system probably cannot be projected with that level of accuracy. Second, the costs of obtaining the last few degrees of accuracy will be greater than the potential savings from that accuracy. We have recently been fortunate in working with some extremely explicit large-scale personnel cost figures,[2] but we would not have proposed the cost-gathering effort (and expense) for the sole purpose of our single-application automated systems study alone.

The value of the current operations' cost data lies in the use of cost levels as a type of benchmark; current costs are a measure of hard data to be used in evaluating proposals for a new automated system, and in evaluating the system once installed and operational.

It is important to note that the process of data collection, or observations of operations, can result in changes in the processes observed (the "Hawthorne effect" and more subtle variations). For this reason it is important to obtain the benchmark cost data before any of the changes related to the new system are implemented or discussed with staff. The observer will change the process somewhat by observation, and this effect cannot be removed entirely, but it is much worse if the "observer" is actively involved in changing processes while studying their costs and procedures. As noted above, one element to analyze is the use of revised procedures within an existing function. One must resist the temptation to do the revisions before measuring the starting point. (Conversely, evaluations often assign benefits or cost reductions to new automated systems which are in fact nothing more than revisions of procedures which could have been accomplished with the manual system. If the cataloging department saves money by eliminating underlining of subject headings with a red pen, the cost saving cannot be attributed to the installation of the OCLC terminal.)

The following major cost elements should be collected to provide benchmark information for the evaluation process:

1. *Workload or demand.* Estimates can be provided from historical data for each item processed through the system. Because of the relatively large number of items in libraries' files, and because of the long historical time period most files represent, sophisticated sampling should be employed to ensure that historical data and current practice are related.
   The objective of this element is to determine long-range trends in growth patterns and to determine the patterns of work-flow or demand over shorter periods. The second step is of particular importance because of the wide variations in demand or work-flow which characterize much library activity.
2. *Definition of process.* Current procedures must be analyzed to determine what work steps are actually involved; these may be assumed to have a tenuous relation to written work procedures or job descriptions. At a minimum, event frequencies estimated without measurement of actual experience may be considerably in error. Average times for each event may be obtained by sampling, time-and-motion studies, or diary methods.
   At this point it is well to mention a resource which can and should be used for many cost procedures: plagiarism. A wide variety of detailed library cost studies have been published. Those who work with them can cite limits in each, and it is easy to identify areas where more needs to be done, but the cumulative information available is very much greater than was available a decade ago. In an individual library environment, if a piece of outside cost data looks reasonable in terms of limited local experience, it may be useful. If a number of independent pieces all confirm the initial local effort, do not be distracted in your evaluation process by the conviction that "our library is different." Use what is available and husband your resources for the next two steps in development and evaluation: evaluating that "soft" data and reviewing your local external environment.
3. *Defining interactions.* Independent of the specific procedures currently being followed, certain systematic interactions are taking

place which define the task being studied. These consist of a set of human interactions with: (a) other staff, (b) manual resources, and (c) computer-based resources. The system design will force a change in this mix. It is important to understand its present cost structure in order to predict these changes.

4. *Determining manpower requirements.* Tangible cost benefits from the implementation of an automated system have been most readily found through resulting changes in the mix of manpower skills. That is, while it is seldom realistic to project staff reductions, replacement of expensive staff by less expensive staff can be obtained for many functions. Therefore, it is necessary to define work rates and work standards for tasks through the methods cited above.
5. *Resource costs.* To staff costs must be added measures for unit hardware, software, and development costs for current activities. This consideration should include alternative costs for operation of current functions, i.e. leasing vs. buying equipment, etc.

Each of the five areas outlined should be examined in such a way that comparable information can be obtained about the present operating costs and projected systems costs. Otherwise we may have a four-way mix of automated oranges, manual apples, manual oranges, and automated apples—a fruit salad of analysis.

It is important to establish which "hard data" (as illustrated by costs in this discussion) properly belong in what Learman has called "the domain of analysis," or "the sum of all valid areas of measurement."[3] Learman outlines criteria for including information within a domain of analysis as:

> a) an identifiable, definable input and output for each application to be included; b) some proposed benefit which can be quantified for the proposed change; and c) some functional relationship or equivalence between an application in the current system and in the new system.[4]

Information which does not meet these criteria are outside Learman's "domain" and in general belong in our classification of "soft information." Unfortunately, many of the things management wants to know about a potential automated system lie in the area of "soft" information for most libraries undertaking current projects.

Soft Information

There are two reasons that information is "soft" from the manager's point of view: (1) either the questions being asked have not been defined fully, or (2) the resources do not exist to provide hard data on properly defined questions. For example, "How satisfied is the user of the library?"

A "hard" answer cannot be provided even with unlimited research funds until an agreed-upon definition of satisfaction is provided. An example of the second reason is the inability of most libraries to provide classic time-and-motion analysis on repetitive library tasks in order to obtain very precise operating marginal labor costs. We will discuss two areas of "soft" information which may be considered at the stage of program development—the evaluation of related library activities in other library systems and the evaluation of user needs, demands, or desires.

It is natural for a library to want to draw on the experience of other systems when planning a major change such as represented by almost any automated system. The insistence by some staff on the uniqueness of the local library is not often shared by the library administrator wishing to minimize risk and maximize results in an automated system. Those who are implementing pioneering systems soon become familiar with a wide range of visitors, national and international, who have arrived "to see how it is working at...."

Unfortunately, while library functions can be described as "the same" at some very broad level—everyone acquires, accounts for, catalogs, and circulates materials—these operations today differ widely due to the variety of institution goals they support and the level of instructional resources available. To obtain relatively "hard" information about, for instance, the performance and costs of a potential vendor's circulation system, would require that the library studied be similar in all features to the library looking for information.

In addition, it is increasingly true that the more successful automated systems are broader in scope and more complex than the earlier traditional automated functions. Many systems stretch the state of the technology, or at least the state of deliverable products. While it is true that those involved in the operation of such systems find it increasingly possible to evaluate and share each others' efforts (the transfer of the University of California, Berkeley, serials KWIC publication programs to Harvard is an example), such sharing does not suggest the evaluation process is simple for libraries without specialized internal systems staffs.

In our opinion, the reliance on other libraries' reported experiences, or on the results of "whirlwind" survey tours, are sufficiently limited to be a marginal source of reliable information to most libraries. Intelligent review of library and information technology literature can provide good indications of what is feasible, but a one-day site visit anywhere can provide only the politically useful "soft" information confirming that the site visited does in fact perform the functions the written literature claimed for it.

If libraries were organized as businesses or as mission-oriented federal agencies, they might have ongoing, patron-level, market research programs. Few libraries have any specific "hard" information beyond the demographic level, and no major library system in the United States yet admits to an ongoing program in this area. The efforts that do exist are concerned primarily with measuring patron "satisfaction" with a particular program (a film service, SDI awareness, etc.) or with patron reaction to a specific change in procedures such as the remote storage of little-used materials. This type of program evaluation is a limited effort which has little relationship to the general goals of the library, and thus is of limited value as input to management evaluation. Furthermore, it is often difficult to evaluate patron reaction to automated library services. The more basic measurements are obvious without consulting the patron; cutting in half the time required for charging a book can be measured readily in terms of staff savings, and some proportionate patron benefit can be assumed. As services move beyond housekeeping tasks, however, and into changes in patron access to the collection (new catalogs and automated reference services), evaluation of the effect of change becomes more difficult.

One problem with attempting to gain even "soft" information about patrons is the complexity of the behavioral science research which is required in order to obtain even minimally dependable answers. The number and variety of potential users are considerable (professional and clerical staff, casual and research patrons, young and old, minorities, students and businessmen, and the important majority group, nonusers). An added factor is the variation in use of the library over time (school years, seasons) which demands long-term measurement. The most complex problem, however, is that when dealing with planning for automated services, it is almost impossible to project accurately a potential service in a patron interview. Both patrons and the staff find it difficult to choose among equally unknown alternatives.

Where direct information can support the evaluation of a specific automated system proposal, it should be obtained. For instance, one could reasonably expect to obtain direct answers to the question, "How often do you use another library, and which one?" appropriately written out for presentation to patrons at a circulation desk. The answers could be quite relevant in evaluating the capability of an automated circulation system to maintain either (1) local-branch patron verification files, or (2) systemwide patron verification files. If a library's patrons used other branches in the system heavily, the latter option would be preferable.

Such limited evaluations of patron service will be replaced in most libraries by more abstract measures of services presently provided and to be included in a new automated service. For instance, Orr and his colleagues[5] have developed a general scheme of library services which includes a methodology for measuring collection, document delivery capability, and a services inventory. It is practical and efficient for most library administrators to accept the basic outline of services provided by Orr (which includes providing documents, citations, answers, work space, and instruction, along with a miscellaneous class) and then to base their library's evaluation process on measures of these arbitrarily defined services. The alternative is for the local library to mount a public services behavioral research effort. The model for the library which does have some research capabilities and is not totally satisfied with the conclusions of others is available in the work of Ben-Ami Lipetz at Yale,[6] where a relatively limited scope of information was thoroughly documented from card catalog users. By keeping the scope of the research effort to a focus on "What did you want to find in the card catalog when you approached it?" rather than the much broader "What do you want in the library?" Lipetz produced perhaps the single most useful piece of research regarding user practice in the last decade.

Definition of the Technical Environment

At this stage in the automated system's program, the library will have reviewed what can reasonably be found out about its present operations and the demands upon them, in terms of both "hard" data, such as costs, and "soft" data, such as patron market research. The most significant pitfalls, however, come in evaluating, from inside the organization, the technical resources available to the library to accomplish its goals. Various types of limits will be found to exist:

1. *Institutional:* the organization of the library within the parent organization; authority of the library over other related resources such as the computer center or library-like agencies within the parent organization; contractual or other ties to other libraries.
2. *Facilities:* availability of computer facilities; their type, configuration, and suitability for the peculiar data processing and transmission needs of library applications; policies regarding use of various computer languages; transmission links with other organizations, etc.
3. *Staff:* within the library and other related agencies in the parent organization, evaluation of the available staff's knowledge with regard to all phases of the required effort (systems analysis and design, programming, daily operations); staff ability to train others in the library and support user education; ability of the library to recruit, add, or train staff if required.
4. *File conversion:* relation of conversion for one application to future use for others; technical standards; use of in-house, vendor, or library network resources for conversion.
5. *Management priorities:* limits set by the parent organization or by

the library management which restrain certain applications (e.g., "all service shall be provided without charge"); availability of other resources which support cooperative development.

6. *Finances:* ability for financing capital investments in equipment, data conversion, and program start-up; sources for supporting operating expenses, including internal systems staff.

The end result of all this activity is to provide the management information necessary for the specification of an automation program. Evaluation of each step is determined by the adequacy of input for each of these areas: (1) decision criteria for internal vs. external development, (2) priorities for implementation of subprograms, (3) staffing projections, and (4) cost-benefit analysis. The process should result in the ability to use information gathered to write detailed program specifications, which can be used as a basis for "requests for proposals" and evaluation of vendor proposals.

Program Implementation

The first step in implementation is often described as the "make-or-buy" decision; this is the choice between internal development of the automated system and contract outside development. In the practical sense, outside contractors should be defined to include the parent organization's data processing department, as well as independent vendors. The make-or-buy decision implies the evaluation of the performance capabilities of each type of resource (internal or contract) and in fact generally involves the evaluation of specific programs or services available from individual contractors. It must be recognized that for some library systems this step is functionally nonexistent or trivial. Local circumstances may include an administrative edict requiring all agencies within an organization to use the services of the organization's data processing department. In this case the library is mandated to buy from a specific vendor. Conversely, the first review of library and parent organization resources may demonstrate clearly that no necessary resources are available. In this case, independent sources are mandated.

The improper matching of internal and external resources has probably been responsible for more outright disasters in library automation applications than any other factor. When either good internal staff are burdened by poor computer access, a lack of competent staff leads to little control over vendor programs, or the library and the organization's data processing staff are competing for priorities, one can expect only minimally operational applications. Thus, it is prudent for the library's management to go through the processes of evaluating the implementation even if the choice of resources is forced administratively rather than occurring from exercise of library evaluations. It may be helpful the second time. If freedom of choice is available, the make-or-buy decisions can proceed using the library's choice of the basic management techniques outlined in Table 1. If freedom of choice is not available, then "make" or do nothing.

In buying a contract service or product, there is a general distinction between standard and custom services. Real economies of scale are to be found in the design and delivery of standard services from computer systems to a large number of user libraries. Unfortunately, standardization of operations among most libraries has not progressed much beyond acceptance of the location for the rod hole in the catalog card. As a result, even the better-designed "standard" automated services tend to become "customized" over a period of time because of individual library customer needs or expressed desires.

Potential cost savings are one advantage of a standard contract service or product. A second benefit is that unless your library is the first customer, it is possible to determine that the described product is actually working. A third, and nontrivial, benefit is that the nature of the completed product is such that it can be fully specified, whereas a custom-designed product almost always suffers from some nonspecified discrepancies in expectations during development.

On balance, the evaluation of a system's performance is markedly easier if the system is a replication or transfer of a product or service installed elsewhere. The difficult point is to determine when seemingly innocent and trivial "local changes" transform the project from a standard to a custom system.

In evaluating make-or-buy choices, it will be necessary to evaluate closely the technological trends which define the technical environment of the proposed system. This paper has no room to discuss such important technical issues as microcomputers and value-added networks. It is perhaps worth observing that library automation efforts have more often "stretched" the state of computer technology than is expected by many in the computer or data processing profession. The development of extended character sets for computer printing and CRT display, the handling of very large files on-line for searching, and the use of commercial "light-pen" data entry devices are all examples from recent years. This situation places the library staff evaluating a project in the difficult situation of not wanting to design around obsolete equipment, but at the same time wanting to avoid the risks inherent in unproven technology. No simple method or formula will replace the use of knowledgeable specialists in analyzing the technology.

There are, however, some general guidelines which might be helpful in evaluating make-or-buy options:

1. *Fit your measures to your application.* The vendor procedures for hardware maintenance and error-correction are much more important in a circulation system than in a book catalog production service.

2. *Think of the next three projects.* If the short-term advantage of buying a standard circulation system is negated by the inability of that system to accept input from a later automated bibliographic system, the "standard" product may have saved your library little over making a custom product.
3. *Separate the application and the data base.* Over the past decade, probably the largest single waste of library automation efforts has come from the improperly evaluated development of a local library data base for a specific purpose, later found to be inappropriate for other uses or further implementation on different equipment. In evaluation, consider the development of the data base per se as a separate project from the initial application; but do force evaluation of the data base creation rather than just assuming that "then we can do anything."

Evaluation of Implementation

Evaluating an automated project must be organized before the actual commitments to the program are made. If there is a single element of measuring the performance of a computer-based library application which is different from other data processing applications, it is the breadth of evaluation skills which may be required to assess the success of the project. This is partly because of practical problems in information handling and retrieval posed by large library files and processing demands, but it is also partly due to the complex and generally unevaluated set of cataloging procedures and administrative rules which have grown up in most libraries over a period of years.

It is redundant to insist that the first job of an evaluation effort should be to measure the performance of the present library system which is to be replaced. It is still common, however, to find situations where this practice has not been followed. For instance, during the first three years of on-line operations of the OCLC cataloging system, virtually no studies were published and documented in the literature regarding the effect of that resource on local library catalog departments.

There are at least seven discrete sets of evaluation skills which are likely to be required in implementing and evaluating all but the most basic automated project: (1) administrative and managerial; (2) business and financial; (3) department or function operations; (4) computer and data processing, telecommunications; (5) micrographics and publishing; (6) information science and technology; and (7) market evaluation-user needs. It would be a broad library staff which would supply the range of talents to direct a performance evaluation task. It is necessary in all but the largest libraries for the library administration to draw on a group of resources to evaluate properly the success of a project. This does not particularly suggest the development of a committee to manage a project—generally a disastrous approach—but rather the periodic use of a number of persons representing special skills to review plans and performance. There are five general sources of such skills, each with its advantages and disadvantages.

1. *Library staff.* There is no substitute for involving staff who will be even marginally affected by the new system in the planning and evaluation (not all affected staff, but some representative from each class of staff). However, it must be recognized that staff in a particular department are not necessarily the most competent to evaluate the library's overall goals for a project.
2. *Parent or sister agencies.* Departments in the university, or agencies in public government, can often provide a most useful backup in evaluation. This is often a resource underutilized by library administrations where past experience has been, "...they don't understand library operations." While this statement is true enough historically, in the tight funding atmosphere of the 1970s the effort would seem to be politically most valuable.
3. *User groups.* Less is known about the practice and desires of library users than about any other element affecting design and function of an automated system. While formal and scientifically valid user studies are quite expensive and beyond the resources of most libraries, informal support and advice from politically well-chosen groups of users can be effective in stopping irrelevant design features. The staff is also a special user group of most automated systems, and their special problems as users should be considered in a manner separate from the authority of the system to control their activities as employees.
4. *Consultants.* A prejudiced view from the consultant's perspective is that an outside formal consultant (or one who is not affiliated with the organization and is paid under a formal contract or agreement) can save a project time and money if one or more of the following is needed: (a) education regarding information technology and the state of practice of specific applications; (b) budgeting and planning for a practical and feasible implementation and project design; (c) design expertise in information storage and retrieval, particularly in non-traditional methods; and (d) management review regarding the organization for, and implementation of, a project plan. A limiting factor is that the use of a consultant for a very short period of time generally does not allow for development of very specific guides and recommendations; from one to six man-months during the entire project period is a reasonable level of involvement for many major projects. Thus the use of consultants can be expensive; a reasonable budget might be 5-10 percent of the project effort.

5. *Vendors.* There is some tendency in the library profession to treat the vendor as an adversary whose primary goal is plundering the budget of the local library, particularly if the vendor is a commercial firm. The nature of the library profession makes this an unwarranted assumption; librarians as much as any other group of professional public agency employees have an extensive and intensive communications network. Poor or misrepresented service to a library rapidly becomes known to the library community as a whole. The vendor can be an extremely helpful resource in the planning and evaluation of a system. Control is, of course, necessary and contracts are discussed below to that end; do not, however, exclude the vendor from professional staff evaluation meetings unless the agenda is specifically a review of his performance.

Contracts in Performance Evaluation

A proper contract stripped of legal and purchasing verbiage, which necessarily gets added in formal bid contracts, is simply a written specification of what is expected from the automated project. A vendor contract and an internal-project planning document are the same from an operating point of view; the sanctions for nonperformance simply differ.

The library should draw up a contract whether working with internal development, a sister data processing agency, or an outside vendor. It should include all specified products and services ("deliverables") and should include schedules and procedures of modification. The contract is the sole place where the adversary approach to performance should prevail. A vendor contract is a legal document; for agreements within the library's organization, a contract is the definition of commitments.

Do not include undefined, hoped-for goals in the contract document unless both parties to the contract clearly understand that no evaluation of performance is possible on those elements. It may be useful, particularly in bid contracts, to specify open-ended options to be specified mutually at a later time (e.g., in a book catalog contract, "and the production of such special indexes as shall be mutually agreed upon"). This technique is basically useful only for providing some extra flexibility and avoiding rebid situations for minor changes. It cannot specify price and performance on uncompleted products. On the other hand, do include in a contract specific performance benchmarks: maximum number of seconds per circulation transaction, maximum number of days turnaround for book catalog production, etc. It should, however, be recognized that sanctions specified for nonperformance are basically only protections against disaster, and not a useful operating management tool. Any benchmarks specified should only have legal status when measured in actual operating conditions.

The function of a contract (particularly a public bid) is to measure price and performance among qualified vendors, and to eliminate nonqualified responses. The bid document will not serve this function unless the library specifies clearly in the document what bases are used for evaluation of vendors. This means the library must investigate sufficiently in order to identify the truly qualified vendors before sending out the bid specification. Then the bid design must be reviewed to make sure it does not arbitrarily exclude qualified vendors and does not allow responses from nonqualified vendors.

If it is not possible to determine what is available a priori, it is the practice of some agencies (particularly large federal operations) to issue a "request for proposal," in response to which vendors can describe their services and suggest actions for the agency. This is only practicable for the largest libraries who can invest considerable staff time and funding for a major contract, because of the cost of responding to an open-ended "RFP." Most libraries are well advised to invest their own time talking personally to vendors before issuing a bid document.

There are at present three general problems with evaluating contracts for the provision of automated library services:

1. *Nothing is identical.* It is unlikely that two responses to a contract specification will be identical. We simply do not have a standard set of descriptions of library operations, much less a standard set of computer applications programs. This situation can be expected to persist in the next decade, thus providing plenty of chances for consultants and others to attempt to make something other than lemons from the apples and oranges available with which to work.
2. *Competition is sparse.* Only in the area of contract book (or microform) catalog services can one find as many as ten organizations providing nationwide services to libraries. We will perhaps see three to five on-line network systems become available within the next five years, but generally with regional emphasis. In acquisitions there are a few software or turnkey systems that are beginning to replace a previous generation of simple data collection devices.
3. *Reality is elusive.* Most libraries without special expertise will gain little in investigating standard contract products through the route of field visits or correspondence with vendors' user libraries. The problem is even more difficult if the library chooses to develop a custom product with a contractor (agency or vendor) without previous experience.

When Disaster Looms

The best early warning system of real trouble in a system implementation is the experience that comes from having lived through one or more previous disasters. In the absence of that chastening background, some brief rules may help. Disaster may be on the way if:

1. You can't understand in English what you are buying in the computer system.
2. You can't get a firm schedule with real dollar penalties for late delivery.
3. You can't get firm estimates on processing or related operating costs.
4. Nothing comes out of any step of development for more than three months.
5. Your developer tells you library problems are really very simple!

Review of Program Operation

So far we have been considering performance measures as they relate to the planning and implementation of an automated system. We have been concerned with the potential of the projected system to meet the institution's goals in terms of tasks and costs. Now we want to measure the results of all this activity—measurement which can be accomplished through review of program operation.

This review is only possible if we have gone through the previously described rigorous procedures—defining operations, determining costs, and formulating goals—prior to the implementation of the new system. Without having completed these steps, we would not only be trying to compare manual apples with automated oranges, but with hybrid strawberries as well. The purpose of this review is to give us a measure of the success or failure of the new, automated system in achieving the goals set for the program.

Success or failure can be measured in three ways which may be assigned proportionately to the desired goals: costs, performance, and benefits. The easiest measurement is that of costs, particularly if we have applied standard methodology to the determination of manual cost elements (workload, staffing, processes, resources, etc.) which may serve as benchmarks against which to measure costs of these same elements in an automated system. Similarly, actual development costs can be accurately determined and measured against projected development costs and costs of comparable systems which have been reported in the literature. This type of hard data can give management a gross estimate of the success or failure of the new system within the framework of established budgetary limitations.

The more difficult task is to obtain and, if possible, to quantify soft data regarding the success or failure of the system in achieving program goals at other than the cost level. (We are deliberately including the element of failure which is conspicuously absent in the literature, yet potentially is of even more informational value than the many records of successful, or at least viable, operation.) These soft data fall into the categories of performance and benefit, which have been characterized by Orr[7] as measures of capability, utilization (service loads) and value. The first of these two are based on criteria which can indeed be measured through the answers to such questions as: What is the number of file items searched in a specified time? What is the number of outputs produced in a specified time? What is the number of files eliminated? There are many more questions which knowledgeable library staff can readily identify.

Benefit, or value, is a more difficult concept to quantify, although Orr suggests a way to do so by stating: "the value of a service must ultimately be judged in terms of the beneficial effects accruing from its use as viewed by those who sustain the costs."[8] While agreeing with Orr in a pragmatic sense, we feel that the difficulty in quantifying benefit lies in the fact that it is a function of the user rather than of the library or its resources. For instance, one of the projected benefits of an automated circulation system is the shortening of queuing time at the charge desk—a benefit for the user rather than the library staff member who must man the desk no mater what. In an academic environment it is possible to calculate the average faculty salary and thus assign a dollar value to the time spent by the faculty member in checking out material. But what of the student?

In order to obtain hard data in this area, we must turn to the "forced quantification of uncertainty" whereby we assign relative values to discernible benefits which are usually expressed in percentages of total cost.

What is it worth to us, the library administration, to save the patron time in checking out a book or to provide the patron with item availability information? Do these benefits account for 5 percent or 50 percent of the total cost of the automated circulation system? The answers to these and similar questions will enable us to calculate a dollar value for what are usually described as intangible benefits.

This forced quantification of uncertainty provides us with additional measure by which we may assess the success or failure of the program in achieving its specified goals, both at the time of implementation and on a continuing basis. This procedure can also provide another dimension to the traditional historical data collection by libraries which may be used in the planning of new and related programs. On a secondary level, quantification can provide a format for reporting to institution management in a manner intelligible to those who know—or care to know—little concerning the library's internal operations.

Limits of Performance Measurement

Passing mention has been given to the various techniques employed for the performance evaluation of computer systems. Most of these—mixes, benchmarks, etc.—are based on modeling and simulation, which in turn demand the creation of software which can consume the available funds to such an extent that none are left for the testing phase. This is probably one of the major reasons that such techniques have not been extensively employed in the evaluation of library automation efforts. Another reason is that such techniques primarily measure the performance of the equipment and not of the system as a whole, which is our primary interest. Simulation has, however, been employed in those highly structured situations where it was appropriate—as in the NELINET and OCLC studies of user terminal behavior—and where sufficient financial and technical resources were available. In this paper we have concentrated on those techniques and methodologies which are readily available to library staff without extensive technical expertise, large sums of money, or the ability to mount parallel operations. In general, these techniques and methodologies are applicable to the management of any library operation.

It should be obvious that the extent of cost and task analysis and performance measurement proposed in this paper will consume a fair proportion of the library's resources, both man-hours and dollars. What has been presented here is a model which can and will be adapted to the resources and needs of the individual institution relative to the resources required for the planning and implementation of an automated system. Analysis can become an end in itself, but we are probably beyond the point where we can afford such luxuries as full-time systems staffs devoted to this process. We should like to summarize briefly and end by paraphrasing Plato in saying that "the library which is not examined is the library not worth automating."

REFERENCES

1. Swanson, Rowena W. "Design and Evaluation of Information Systems," *Annual Review of Information Science and Technology* 10:43-101, 1975.

2. Butler, Brett, *et al. Improving Public Library Access; The Los Angeles County Public Library System Access Study, Final Report.* Los Altos, Calif., R&D Consultants, 1975.

3. Learman, I. "Cost-benefit Analysis in the Design and Evaluation of Information Systems," *AFIPS Fall Joint Computer Conference, Proceedings* 39:470, 1971.

4. *Ibid.*

5. Orr, Richard H., *et al.* "Development of Methodologic Tools for Planning and Managing Library Services," *Bulletin of the Medical Library Association* 56:235-67, July 1968; and 56:380-403, Oct. 1968.

6. Lipetz, Ben-Ami. "Catalog Use in a Large Library," *Library Quarterly* 42:129-39, Jan. 1972.

7. Orr, Richard H. "Measuring the Goodness of Library Services; A General Framework for Considering Quantitative Measures," *Journal of Documentation* 29:315-32, Sept. 1973.

8. *Ibid.*, p. 318.

ADDITIONAL REFERENCES

Balke, K.G. "Person-centered Measurement." In *Proceedings of Computer Science and Statistics* (7th Annual Symposium on the Interface). Ames, Iowa, Iowa State University, Statistics Laboratory, 1973, pp. 86-91.

Evans, Edward, *et al.* "Review of Criteria Used to Measure Library Effectiveness," *Bulletin of the Medical Library Association* 60:102-10, Jan. 12 1972.

Hamburg, Morris, et al. *"Library Objectives and Performance Measures and their Use in Decision Making,"* Library Quarterly 42:107-28, Jan. 1972.

Holt, George A., and Stern, H.C. "Cost-benefit Evaluation of Interactive Transaction Processing Systems," *AFIPS National Computer Conference* 44:687-94, 1975.

Janes, J.D.W. "Computer-based Decision Aids: The Evaluation Problem," *Sloan Management Review* 16:17-29, Spring 1975.

Keen, P.G.W. "Computer-based Decision Aids: The Evaluation Problem," *Sloan Management Review* 16:17-29, Spring 1975.

Lucas, Henry C. "Performance Evaluation and Monitoring," *Computing Surveys* 3:79-91, Sept. 1971.

Raffel, Jeffrey A. "From Economic to Political Analysis of Library Decision Making," *College & Research Libraries* 35:412-23, Nov. 1974.

HUGH FOLK
Professor of Economics
Institute of Labor and Industrial Relations
University of Illinois
Urbana-Champaign

The Impact of Computers on Book and Journal Publication

Rising wages have made the cost of composition and printing editions of a few thousand copies exorbitant. Rising book and journal prices have contributed to the rising operating expenses of libraries. At the same time, the volume of scientific and technical literature is increasing rapidly and the publication and library system is increasingly incapable of satisfying user needs.

Electronic publication of scientific and technical literature is technically feasible. One machine-readable copy of a document may be stored in a computer and accessed at any remote location by a user with a computer terminal. Current costs of preparing a machine-readable text, storing it on a computer, communicating with the remote computer, and computer time for the user to read or print the document are low enough that, for many applications in scientific publishing, a computer-based system may be less expensive than the existing paper-and-ink system. Rapidly decreasing computer and communications costs indicate that electronic publication will be increasingly cost-effective compared to alternative systems.

The benefits of a comprehensive electronic system for scientific and technical publishing are substantial. Not only would such a system be more complete and less expensive than conventional publication and distribution, but it also would be more accessible. Many users who do not now have access to the scientific literature could use the system. An electronic system would increase scientific productivity; not only would the scientist spend less time learning about what has been done, but he/she would obtain much more current information than is now available. Moreover, a computer-based scientific information system could provide a medium for two-way communications between users that would be more convenient and effective than the telephone or mail service.

PUBLICATION OF SCIENTIFIC BOOKS AND JOURNALS

Most scientific literature is published by professional societies, universities, and government, with few scientific books and journals selling more than a few thousand copies. Scientific literature is complex in terms of composition; it is characterized by equations, tables, and diagrams, the composition cost of which may exceed printing and distribution costs. The amount of scientific literature is growing rapidly. The stock of scientific publication has been estimated to increase at 7 percent annually;[1] the total number of journals is increasing at 4 percent per year.[2]

The growth of scientific literature threatens to overwhelm readers. Libraries, cramped for space and short of money, cannot hope to provide complete coverage of the growing literature. Indexing and abstracting by computer may identify what is in the literature, but this makes the tasks of libraries more complex.[3] Interlibrary loan and photoduplicates are increasingly used to provide missing documents, but seekers of current literature frequently pursue the author by mail and request a reprint. Because of journals such as *Current Contents*, a parallel system of author-to-reader distribution has forced upon authors the burden and cost of distributing their work.[4]

A huge literature of technical reports has also emerged;[5] unreviewed, unread, and unsung (at least by promotion committees), technical reports are cited with increasing frequency. Most are not indexed and consequently are difficult to find, but federal government-supported research reports are increasingly included in the National Technical Information Service (NTIS), are indexed, and are readily obtainable as microfiche, photocopy, or magnetic tape.

Attempts to stifle the growth of the literature create more problems than they solve. Proposals to tighten reviewing and to exclude literature from journal publication are idealistic but unrealistic. Authors must publish even if they have nothing to say and, if necessary, they will create new journals.

Attempts to lower the costs of publication by using microfiche, separates, or abstract or condensed journals simply fragment the literature further and increase the gadgets and oddly shaped cabinets in the library.[6] These new media also increase the pressures on authors for direct distribution.

A scientific information system that is complete, unified, rapid, and inexpensive is the goal. Many people claim that by the 1990s such a computerized scientific information system will exist. Computers are considered to be too dumb, too small, and too costly to do the job today. They are thought to be too dumb to process the multilevel math, tables, and diagrams that fill technical writing, too small to store and access the trillions of characters required, and too expensive to replace the existing paper/ink and film system.

Many who have worked with computers are acutely aware of their limitations, but those who are involved in the development of new computer systems realize that large complex systems are being created at an accelerating pace. Lockheed Information Systems offers in DIALOG a remarkable set of bibliographical indexes usable interactively by telephone or Telenet. The LEXIS system of Mead Data Central, Inc., provides on-line retrieval of legal text for several states. Large data-base applications in business are widespread; some firms have hundreds of terminals accessing a central computer and processing millions of transactions daily. Moreover, computer costs are decreasing rapidly. It is these recent developments that make an economical, computer-based scientific information system possible.

COMPOSITION OF SCIENTIFIC BOOKS AND JOURNALS

Between Gutenberg in 1450 and Mergenthaler in 1886, hand composition experienced no significant technological change. Slug casting, or hot-metal composition, reduced production costs sharply. In 1890, Alfred Marshall's *Principles of Economics* sold for $4, a worker's weekly wage, while in 1936, Keynes's *General Theory of Employment, Interest, and Money* sold for $2, a worker's daily wage.

Book and journal prices remained remarkably stable for the first half of the twentieth century, material and labor price increases apparently offset by increases in productivity. From 1967 to 1974, the price of hardcover books increased by 67 percent,[7] and from 1967 to 1975, U.S. periodicals increased by 130 percent, with even greater increases for chemistry and physics (214 percent) and for engineering (166 percent). The large increases in the cost of scientific and technical periodicals result from their typographical complexity.

Cost increases during the past two decades would have been even greater had not publishing technology improved. Offset printing has made it easy to reproduce simple typescript, but typescript is ugly. Lines are unjustified, letters are usually the same width, and footnotes and tables are unattractive. Strike-on composition with even margins was made possible with justifying typewriters, and more sophisticated strike-on compostion is possible with new devices such as magnetic card typewriters, computer terminals, or computer line-printers.

Strike-on composition is inferior in speed and elegance to photocomposition, which can solve all of the typographical problems of the compositor. Subscripts, superscripts, non-Roman alphabets, and several type sizes are readily composed. Phototypesetters are normally driven from magnetic tape produced by a computer.

Strike-on and phototypesetter composition, or "cold-type" composition, have been widely adopted. At its best, the quality equals that of hot type. For pure text composition the cost can be as little as $3 or $4 a page, or comparable to typewritten text composition. A typist working with a computer text editor can produce copy with speed and accuracy. With the economy and speed of offset printing, press runs of a few hundred copies can be quite inexpensive.

Offset printing has contributed to the growth of scientific publication. In the 1960s, Praeger, using typewriter composition, produced a number of books from doctoral dissertations and technical reports. In the late 1960s, Heath Lexington adopted cold copy to produce justified-text books. The first of these were not very attractive—footnotes dangled and white space was uneven—but libraries bought them and the publishers apparently made money.

During the 1960s cold copy was widely adopted by technical publishers. Today, text is set on a phototypesetter, but tables and equations are usually monotyped, proofed and stripped with the text photocopy to produce the page copy.[8] Composition combining photocopy, monotype, and typescript requires several suppliers and is slow and costly.[9] Moreover, the complexity of the process drives production managers wild. (Parisi gives a fascinating history of composition at the American Institute of Civil Engineers.[10])

Publishers agree that a completely computer-based composition system is needed and will take over the market as soon as it becomes available. It need not be inexpensive: publishers want speed and simplicity. Economy is important and would accelerate the adoption of computer photocomposition, but high-quality appearance is necessary.

COMPUTER-BASED COMPOSITION

Computer-based composition produces a single computer file that contains all text, tables, equations, footnotes, references, and page makeup instructions to run an on- or off-line phototypesetter. Several such systems are used commercially to compose scientific journals.[11] The TROFF system developed by Bell Laboratories[12] is used to compose in-house technical reports, documentation, and at least one technical newsletter.[13] This system has several major advantages and represents the current state of the art: (1) it runs on inexpensive computer hardware, (2) it is usable by persons with little training, and (3) it uses an inexpensive phototypesetter. TROFF runs on the UNIX time sharing system developed by Bell Laboratories as a general operating system for the Digital Equipment Corporation PDP 11/45 and 11/70 computers.[14] UNIX includes a powerful context editor that allows a typist to input text at either an on-line terminal or an off-line cassette terminal.[15] The typist inputs equations and table using special programs that can be learned in a few hours.[16] Once in the computer, the draft can be corrected by using special commands, such as *spell*, which looks up every word in an on-line dictionary and produces a list of words not in the dictionary, and *typo*, which uses the rules of English spelling (such as they are) to find possible typographical errors. Other programs have been written by various users to help authors improve their style. A word-frequency command provides a list of words used in a document and a count of how many times each was used. Another program prints the lines in which some troublesome homophones (such as *there/their*) or pet words (such as *obviously* and *clearly*) occur so that a writer can avoid error.

The UNIX typist then inserts commands to provide for centering, underlining, footnoting, equations, tables, indentation and other typographical specifications. The TROFF program then processes the file with text and interspersed command language and produces a decent-looking, justified typescript.

Three kinds of output files can be produced by the TROFF program. Text without footnotes, superscripts, subscripts, or multilevel equations can be printed correctly on a line-printer. Text including these complications can be printed on a special printer, such as a Diablo. Text with phototypesetter commands interspersed can be printed on the phototypesetter.

The emergence of commercial, computer-based phototypesetting means that the day of hot-metal or mixed-mode composition for technical publishers is ending. The availability of machine-readable copy from phototypesetter files suggests that concurrent electronic and printed publication is now possible.

A COMPUTER-BASED SCIENTIFIC INFORMATION SYSTEM

No serious technical problems prevent development of a computer-based scientific information system (SIS). Computer-based photocomposition demonstrates that computers can store and print typographically complex documents.[17] On-line disc systems can store billions of characters, any of which can be accessed in milliseconds. Computers can be accessed remotely by telephone, or interconnected through data-communications networks. Computer time-sharing allows hundreds of users to use the same computer interactively and simultaneously. SIS is technically feasible, but most people think the computer costs are too high to build one now.

SIS, like any storage and retrieval system for scientific documents, must accommodate an enormous volume of material and low usage. Any such system is dominated by the cost of data input and storage, with computer system costs a very small fraction of the total.

Computer-based photocomposition can reduce the cost of data entry substantially. Several publishers, such as the American Institute of Civil Engineers and the American Chemical Society, are now using computer-based photocomposition to print their journals; others, such as the American Institute of Physics, use computer composition for parts of each article, such as title, author, and abstracts. Multiple use of part of the material is increasingly common.[18] Machine-readable abstracts are routinely used in the production of secondary journals and indexes.

It is said that each article in a scientific journal is read ten to twenty times in its life. This statistic depresses authors and computer system designers alike. It hardly seems possible that it would be economical to retain scientific literature of such limited popularity throughout eternity on a computer disc with an access time of a few milliseconds, yet it is.[19]

The telephone is inexpensive for local calls and costly for long distance. Economical electronic publishing requires minimization of the combined storage, communication, and computer cost. Storage costs are minimized with one universally accessible copy on disc, but this requires the use of long-distance telephone lines. To print a 10-page, 50,000-byte article might require five minutes using a common thirty-character-per-second terminal. This could cost from $1 to $5, depending on the locations of the reader and the computer, and the time of day. This is inexpensive compared to costs of $7-$8 for interlibrary loan.

The telephone line can transmit information faster than the terminal can type it, so it is necessary to have either a faster terminal or a local computer to buffer the transmission. Computer networks can reduce the cost of data communications. Each node in the network has a computer which receives messages (or documents) and stores them until the user wants them. Because many users' messages are passing through a communications circuit simultaneously, each message (or "packet") must be labeled with identifying information. Research networks (such as ARPANET) and commercial networks (such as Telenet) using packet-switching technology are operating and obtaining substantial economies in data communications.

Packet-switching networks such as ARPANET and Telenet allow interconnection of dissimilar computers and permit users to send and receive files from remote computers easily. Minicomputers can be interfaced to a network without using any significant part of their memory or sacrificing much of their local processing power.[20] Packet-switching technology makes the cost of data transmission essentially independent of distance or intensity of usage. The user pays for the data actually transmitted plus the cost of occupying a permanent port on the network and users may pay an hourly connect charge to cover the costs of direct terminal access.[21]

Computer time-sharing is a well-established technology, and almost everyone has used such a system or has stood by helplessly while one was being used. Most time-sharing systems operate on medium-sized computers costing several million dollars to support a few dozen simultaneous users. Some systems, such as PLATO IV, support several hundred simultaneous users in sophisticated (but computationally limited) applications. The cost of an hour of computer time is usually based on how much hardware is used, but commercial time on full-sized systems usually averages from $10 to $25 per connect hour. Limited service systems, such as PLATO IV, may be able to provide services at a cost of from $2 to $3 per hour. The development of time-sharing operating systems for low-cost minicomputers promises to reduce general-purpose time-sharing costs to $1-$2 per hour. Special limited-purpose usage, such as that required from printing documents and inputting data, should be somewhat less expensive.[22]

Data input costs are very low for journals using computer-based photocomposition. New disc systems are inexpensive, computer networking provides low-cost communications, and minicomputers can provide low-cost time-sharing services.

A distributed SIS is emerging without any plan or central direction. Not only is DIALOG available on Telenet, but several universities (such as MIT) have computers on the network. Thus, the indexing system and user hosts already are interconnected. All that is necessary for SIS to exist is that one or more publishers place their machine-readable texts on a network computer. An organization such as the American Chemical Society or the Institute of Electrical and Electronic Engineers could make part or all of their future publications available in this manner. Indexes could indicate the articles that were available and the host address. As journal hosts joined the network, a computerized scientific information system would emerge.

IMPACT OF A COMPUTERIZED SCIENTIFIC INFORMATION SYSTEM

A computerized scientific information system is emerging. It promises eventually to cost less and be far more convenient for the user than the existing publishing and library system. Computer cost trends suggest that we should not be niggardly in designing the system. A computerized system with the capability of two-way communications must not merely imitate the paper-and-ink system of today. SIS need not be a limited document storage and retrieval system; for example, a network "mail" system would permit readers to comment on a document and the author to reply.[23] The comments and replies could be linked to the document file so that subsequent readers could be brought up to date on the state of discussion. Authors might also use the system to prepare and submit papers for publication, and editors and referees would use the system to speed publication by on-line reviewing, using the network mail system. The mail facility would permit scientific publication to be quite rapid; for example, a few days would suffice for refereeing, author's corrections, and copy editing. The system would become complete, and a user could access every document in the system from anywhere in the world, and no journal would ever be in the bindery.

Such a system would have at least as much garbage in it as libraries do today—probably more—but the garbage would not clog the system. Computer-based indexing would guide a new breed of scholars to the literature, and users could retrieve everything bearing on a subject they wish to investigate deeply, or skim the cream by requesting only widely cited and reviewed articles. Inaccurate, slovenly, and plagiarized articles would be panned; at last it would be possible for authors to publish and perish at the same time.

The impact of SIS on authors and readers would be revolutionary: no document will be condemned to obscurity, or hidden from a reader who wants it. The impact of SIS on publishers would also be revolutionary. At first they would attempt to collect a copyright fee, but ultimately SIS would become the exclusive system. Nonprofit publishers who are only attempting to cover expenses would find that modest page charges can cover the cost of publication. Journals in hardcover would wither away, until only the table of contents is left as evidence that the editors have approved publication. Finally, libraries would also wither away, their historic duty done. Perhaps we will call the local user host, through which the user accesses the network to read and write, a "library."

Developments in computer-based photocomposition now hold the promise of producing inexpensive photocopy from a single sequential file. In the process of producing this file, electronic publication of scientific literature becomes available as a low-cost alternative to conventional distribution. Recent decreases in the costs of disc storage, time-sharing computers, and the development of computer networking permit cheap storage, access and transmission of text files. As a result, computer composition and electronic publication now appear to be less expensive than conventional publication. To gain these advantages, libraries should be prepared to participate as user sites and to install user network hosts to provide access to the network as electronically published journals become available. Publishers should participate in developing the system by providing machine-readable copies of their publications to experimental and demonstration systems.

The widespread adoption of electronic publishing will herald an important new day in science. The act of publication will become the first step in scientific communication, rather than the last step, as it is too often today. The scientific literature will become unified, reversing the recent trend toward diverse forms of publication. Scientists everywhere will have equal access to the scientific literature, so that the advantages of being in a famous center of research will be substantially lessened. Scientists in obscure universities or poor countries will be able to participate in scientific discourse more readily. When that day finally dawns, scientists will look back on the problems of authors, publishers, and librarians of today with sympathy. Let us hope that they will be grateful for the work that was done to make electronic publishing possible.

REFERENCES

1. Price, Derek J. de Solla. "Citation Measures of Hard Science, Soft Science, Technology, and Nonscience." *In* Carnot E. Nelson and Donald K. Pollock, eds. *Communication Among Scientists and Engineers.* Lexington, Heath Lexington Books, 1970, pp. 3-23.

2. Barr, Diana R. *Trends in Book Production and Prices.* London, National Central Library, 1972, p. 24.

3. Many people believe that computer indexing and abstracting is not very reliable, efficient or cost-effective. Approaches such as Salton's SMART, written in appropriate languages and implemented on appropriate hardware, can be extremely useful. It is important to distinguish between interactive systems which the user can direct and redirect to desired documents, and batch systems in which a once-and-for-all request must be specified. An interactive system can be highly efficient in retrieving all desired documents, and is limited only by the user's imagination in specifying objectives.

4. An author has, perhaps, the right to hope that having paid submission, review or page charges for publishing his article, he has done his part to finance distribution. The heavy cost of distribution by reprints in some fields is burdensome for the author, but it is much more inexpensive for the requester than is interlibrary loan or subscribing to the journal. Requesters seem to expect free, postpaid copies, and sometimes grow abusive when a charge is imposed. As it is, a reader with a stack of prepaid and preprinted postcards can build an excellent library at the expense of the authors.

5. Brearley, Neil. "The Role of Technical Reports in Scientific and Technical Communication," *IEEE Transactions on Professional Communication* PC-16:117-19, Sept. 1973.

6. Bovee, Warren G. "Scientific and Technical Journals on Microfiche," *IEEE Transactions on Professional Communication*, PC-16:113-16, Sept. 1973; and Staiger, David L. "Separate Article Distribution as an Alternative to Journal Publication," *IEEE Transactions on Professional Communication* PC-16:107-12+, Sept. 1973.

7. Brown, Norman B. "Price Indexes for 1975," *Library Journal* 100:1291-95, July 1975.

8. The trouble or expense in setting mathematical equations has led to the exportation of much of the mathematical typesetting to Europe. This is much less expensive for books, but it is obviously impractical for journals that attempt to be current. G. Wroughton of Superior Printing, Champaign, Ill., has developed a highly effective and high-quality phototypesetter (using Alphatype as a foundation) that allows on-line setting of up to eight-level math that is used particularly for mathematical texts.

9. Metzner, A.W. Kenneth. "Multiple Use and Other Benefits of Computerized Publishing," *IEEE Transactions on Professional Communication* PC-18: 274-78, Sept. 1975.

10. Parisi, Paul A. "Composition Innovations at the American Society of Civil Engineers," *IEEE Transactions on Professional Communication* PC-18: 244-73, Sept. 1975.

11. Mack, Paul F. "Lower Composition Costs Through Optical Scanning and Photocomposition," *IEEE Transactions on Professional Communication* PC-18:279-80, Sept. 1975; Metaner, *op. cit.*; and Parisi, *op. cit.*

12. Ossanna, J.F. "TROFF User's Manual." Bell Laboratories internal memorandum, 1974.

13. Lesk, M. "Cheap Typesetters," *SIGLASH Newsletter* 6:14-15, Oct. 1973.

14. Ritchie, Dennis M., and Thompson, Ken L. "The UNIX Time-sharing System," *Communications of the ACM* 17:365-75, July 1974.

15. For a description of several on-line editors and their use, *see* Roistacher, Richard C. "On-line Computer Text Processing: A Tutorial," *Behavior Research Methods & Instrumentation* 6:159-66, 1974.

16. Kernighan, Brian W., and Cherry, Lorinda L. "A System for Typesetting Mathematics," *Communications of the ACM* 18:151, March 1975. Equation typing on other systems is usually difficult or tedious; *see* Korbuly, Dorothy K. "A New Approach to Coding Displayed Mathematics for Photocomposition," *IEEE Transactions on Professional Communication* PC-18:283-87, Sept. 1975.

17. Diagrams and line-drawings can be digitized, stored and printed on printers such as the Diablo or graphics scope terminals. Even half-tones or television frames can be stored and displayed. In terms of storage, a picture is worth considerably more than a thousand words. Doing these things in a commercial system is simply a matter of cost.

18. Metzner, *op. cit.*

19. Suppose one printed volume of a journal costs $25 and is purchased and shelved by 100 libraries at a total cost of $2,500. Storing 100 volumes requires about ten square feet of library floor space or, at current construction costs, about $400. Thus, the capital cost of the volume to the library system is $2,900. A volume is about 5 megabytes (MB), or 1,000 pages of 5,000 bytes (or characters) each. An AED controller and disc system for 536 MB (formatted) costs about $75,000. This system would hold 100 different journals for a cost of $750 per journal. Mass storage devices with much cheaper costs (less than $1/MB) are commercially available, but for a distributed system using minicomputers, a single system will not exceed a few hundred megabytes.

20. For a clear, but technical, discussion of this, *see* Chesson, G. "The Network Unix System." In *Proceedings of the 5th Symposium on Operating Systems Principles*. Austin, Tex., 1975.

21. The current charge for Telenet is about $6/MB and $2/hr. for connect time. A user accessing the network through a user host would pay the connect charge to that host and not the Telenet connect charge. The average cost of host-to-host data transmission is about $7/MB. This cost will be reduced substantially in the future.

22. A Digital Equipment Corporation PDP 11/70, supporting up to thirty-two simultaneous users, with sixty-seven megabytes of AED fast swap disc, 64k words of memory, and hardware and telephone interfaces can be purchased for about $100,000. With the system running unattended, operating, space, and maintenance costs should not be more than $20,000 a year. If 25 percent utilization were achieved (about 60,000 connect hours) the system could break even on a five-year depreciation schedule for about $.67/hr. for connect time. A system with hardware similar to the one described is operating at the University of California, Berkeley, and is informally reported to achieve the operating characteristics specified.

23. This facility exists on many time-sharing systems as a message system. I typed this paper on the Center for Advanced Computation's computer system and sent a message to a colleague to comment on it. He copied the paper from my directory and sent his comments to me overnight. The network mail facility is in constant use over the ARPANET. Every registered user has a mail address, and a message is sent from a user on his own system by typing a command such as "netmain high at Ill-nts" followed by the message or file that is to be sent.

ADDITIONAL REFERENCES

Burchinal, Lee G. "Microforms and Electronic Publication: Emerging Bases for Scientific Communications," *IEEE Transactions on Professional Communication* PC-18:174-76, Sept. 1975.

Licklider, J.C.R. *Libraries of the Future.* Cambridge, Mass., M.I.T. Press, 1965.

Morris, Robert, and Cherry, Lorinda L. "Computer Detection of Typographical Errors," *IEEE Transactions on Professional Communication* PC-18:54-55, March 1975.

Senders, John W. "Information Storage Requirements for the Contents of the World's Libraries," *Science* 141:1067-68, 1963.

Shirrell, Robert. "New Production Options for the Journal Publisher," *IEEE Transactions on Professional Communication* PC-18:150-51, Sept. 1975.

Soma, John T. "The U.S. Computer Industry: An Economic-Legal Analysis of its Major Growth Factors." Ph.D. dissertation prepared for the University of Illinois, 1975.

DOUGLAS S. PRICE
Deputy Director
National Commission on Libraries and
Information Science

Cost Analysis and Reporting as a Basis for Decisions

To avoid any aura of misrepresentation, let me remind you at the outset that I am not a librarian. My background is in information systems, and when I discuss specifics of cost analysis a bit later, most of the examples and techniques will be drawn from that background. However, I would also remind you—perhaps unnecessarily—that libraries are information systems. They are the oldest, the most widespread and the broadest in scope of all information systems, and while they differ markedly from what we generally identify as information systems, their basic purpose is the same and there are many parallels and similarities. Because you are the librarians, I will, on the whole, have to leave it to you to translate what I have to say into the library frame of reference, although I have been told by many librarians over the last five years that it can and should be done.

The Paucity of Usable Library Cost Data

When I first began looking into library cost analysis, I was surprised to find how scant the literature on library costs was. In the course of an exhaustive 1971 study,[1] Charles Bourne was able to locate only about 300 references to library costs. At first glance, 300 may sound like a substantial number, but not when you consider how long we have had libraries, or how much in the way of resources—both human and material—have been devoted to them. The Babylonians had both extensive libraries and cuneiform cost accounting records more than 5,000 years ago, but the earliest reference to the cost of library operations that Bourne could find was a congressional document complaining about the outrageous price charged by the Library of Congress for cataloging Thomas Jefferson's library. (Incidentally, that outrageous price was ten cents per book.)

I suspect that the principal reason libraries have ignored cost analysis until recently stems from the fact that for most of their multimillennial history right up to the present, libraries have been supported by patrons. I do not mean "patron" in the sense of "client," but "patron" in the sense of "patron of the arts," someone who supports an activity simply because it is a good thing to do. Today, the patron is most likely to be a government body, but even the academic libraries and special libraries in industry are supported principally as adjuncts to some other purpose, and not for any quantifiable output they can produce. Therefore, having been shielded from the competition of the marketplace, librarians have, until recently, had little or no incentive to examine their costs of operation.

On the other hand, if someone were to pick up where Bourne left off and scour the literature published since 1971, I would be very surprised if he failed to turn up at least 500 papers and articles on library costs. This sudden surge of interest and activity in library costing is attributable to a number of factors: inflation, proliferation, dessication, competition, and automation. Inflation has sent the costs of library materials, labor, and services soaring. At the same time, more and more materials in a wider variety of media are being made available and are being demanded by users. Meanwhile, federal categorical aid has been drying up or at least badly eroded, while libraries are being forced to compete for revenue-sharing money with such organizations as fire, police, health and sanitation services. Things are bad all over, and they would be positively desperate if the computer were not available with its promise of reducing costs by improving efficiency, promoting sharing, and so on. Notice that I said "promise"—and there is the catch. In the halcyon days of the early 1960s, there was a plethora of promises about the marvelous things computers could do for libraries—and everybody else, for that matter. Unfortunately, performance seldom, if ever, lived up to the promises. Tickets for the automation bandwagon command a high price, and all too many found themselves saddled with ill-conceived and poorly planned automation which, contrary to the promises, increased costs, degraded performance and generally caused problems. Consequently, when the budget crunch of the 1970s came along and librarians began looking at automation for relief, the money managers began asking hard questions such as: Precisely how much money are you going to save? How much is it costing you now? How much is it going to cost to install the system? How long will it take to recover the initial investment? Specifically which line items in your budget are going to be cut as a result of this system and by how much? Which are going to be raised and by how much? In the scramble to find answers to such questions, librarians have collected a large amount of information which has found its way into the literature.

Shortcomings of Published Cost Data

Unfortunately, much—if not most—of this information has been incomplete, inaccurate or ill-conceived. This is not too surprising in view of the relative naiveté of librarians about costs and the circumstances under which the demands for cost information have been made. Almost invariably, the search for cost data has been left until the last stages of the decision process. Consequently, it has been necessary to do what could be done with the information at hand.

In information systems—which, incidentally, are only marginally ahead of libraries in cost analysis—the most common error is that of using gross numbers, e.g., "Our budget last year was $500,000, and we added 50,000 items to the file, so our unit cost was $10.00 per item." In libraries, this is more likely to be fragmented into technical processing budget and items added to the collection, or circulation budget and items circulated. Such numbers may be accurate in that they represent real costs and real volumes, but combining them does not give a real measure of productivity. No library or information system is so homogeneous that a single count can measure its activity. Moreover, what good is such a number? You certainly can not use it to project future costs or to assess past peformance.

Even when the gross number syndrome is avoided, the methods of collecting the detailed cost data are fraught with built-in error. The most common method of separating costs is to ask the employees how they divide their time among various tasks, add up the pieces, match them with some kind of volume count, and produce a unit cost. The principal problem with this approach is its reliance on that most fallible of information storage devices, the human memory. Personally, I would have trouble allocating my time for yesterday, much less last week or last month, and you might also reflect on the common phenomenon of thirty minutes of drudgery looming larger in our minds than a half-day of interesting, challenging work.

Another method which is frequently used—when there is time—is to have everyone keep records for a sample period (usually one month). There is a host of problems with this technique, also. In the first place, if anything is to be usable, someone must sit down and develop a set of categories for recording time and that means walking a razor's edge. Too few categories, and there isn't enough information to be useful; too many, and such a burden is imposed that employees spend more time keeping time than doing work. Then there are the categories "Other" or "Miscellaneous." If you are not careful, you may find that most of your output is "Other." There are also the human problems. You have to teach people to record their time as they go along, and you have to follow up, and follow up, and follow up to make them do it. After all, you are trying to develop a new habit pattern, and you are going to have a lot of occasions when someone forgets to keep track until quitting time and then guesses what the numbers should be. Finally, the procedure of keeping time records will consume some time itself, cutting productivity and making your sample period—which, by the way, has a learning curve in it—thoroughly atypical.

There is one other method for developing unit costs which has been tried occasionally. This is the time study or stopwatch technique. This technique has worked well for the hard goods production industries where the significant operations are repetitive and are all out in the open where they can be watched, but it is totally inappropriate for libraries and information systems, where the important part of the effort is taking place in somebody's head and no two successive items are identical.

All of these costing methods suffer from some common shortcomings, one of the most important of which is the fact that they reflect only a single, usually short, period. If it is a busy period, unit costs will be low; if it is a slack one, unit costs may be high, but there is no way to determine by how much or what the change is with changes in volume. Libraries and information systems have seasonal variations. How do you know if your sample period is typical? What is typical? Finally, except for the gross cost approach, all you are measuring is labor. Even granting that labor is the big piece, it is definitely not the only piece, so you have the problem of figuring out some way of assigning costs for materials, supervision, services, and so on. Usually, these other cost assignments wind up being "finagle factors," which are simply plugged in to make a wrong answer come out "right"; more often than not, something is left out which belongs in, or put in when it shouldn't be. The common habit of lumping everything which can't be easily counted into one or two big categories called "Overhead" or "G&A" (General and Administrative) can completely obscure the costs you are trying to measure. A detailed approach which permits allocating these indirect costs selectively to the benefiting product lines is a lot more work, but it produces much more usable results.

A word about unit costs: I have been discussing unit costs because they provide the best means of relating production to costs. However, unit costs are useless—positively dangerous—unless they are part of a framework which includes all costs, and unless the interpretation of them reflects their true characteristics. It is a fairly comon fallacy to believe that you can multi-ply the unit cost by any volume number to determine the cost of that volume. In any real situation, at least a portion of the costs will remain constant regardless of volume. Building costs and utilities are two examples. In some cases, costs may not vary at all with volume—within limits, of course. I would be surprised if there were not a number of libraries where this would be true if the acquisitions budget were excluded. Normally, a portion of the costs are fixed and a portion are variable. Figure 1 illustrates the three patterns. Curve A, with all costs variable, simply does not exist in the real world. Curve B, with all costs fixed, can occur, but usually means something is wrong. Curve C, with mixed fixed and variable costs, represents the usual real-world situation. The portion below the intercept with the *y*-axis is the fixed costs and the sloped line shows the variability. Of course, the position of the intercept can shift up or down, and the slope of the line can change depending upon the situation. If Curve C is converted from total costs to unit costs, something like Figure 2 results, which dramatizes the variability of unit costs with volume.

Requirements for Usable Cost Information

Let me summarize my criticisms by stating the requirements for valid, useful unit costs:

1. The units of measure of the divisor will be valid measures of the work represented by the costs.
2. They will be logical, arithmetically sound elements of a network which reflects the total costs of the system.
3. They will be the result of careful collection of cost and production information over an extended period of time as a normal part of the production operations.
4. During the extended period, on a regular basis, logical, coherent groups of production items will have been carefully and specifically related to the actual expenditures incurred in producing them.
5. The distribution (allocation) of indirect (nonproduct) costs will have been accomplished against a variety of bases so that, insofar as practical, the burden is carried by the benefiting product lines in proportion to the benefit each receives.
6. Statistical analysis will demonstrate that the unit costs are a mixture of fixed and variable costs, which will result in variations in unit costs proportional to variations in volumes.

THE BUILDING BLOCK CONCEPT

This is a very tough set of criteria to meet, but by borrowing a couple of tricks from the manufacturing industries and modifying them to our pur-

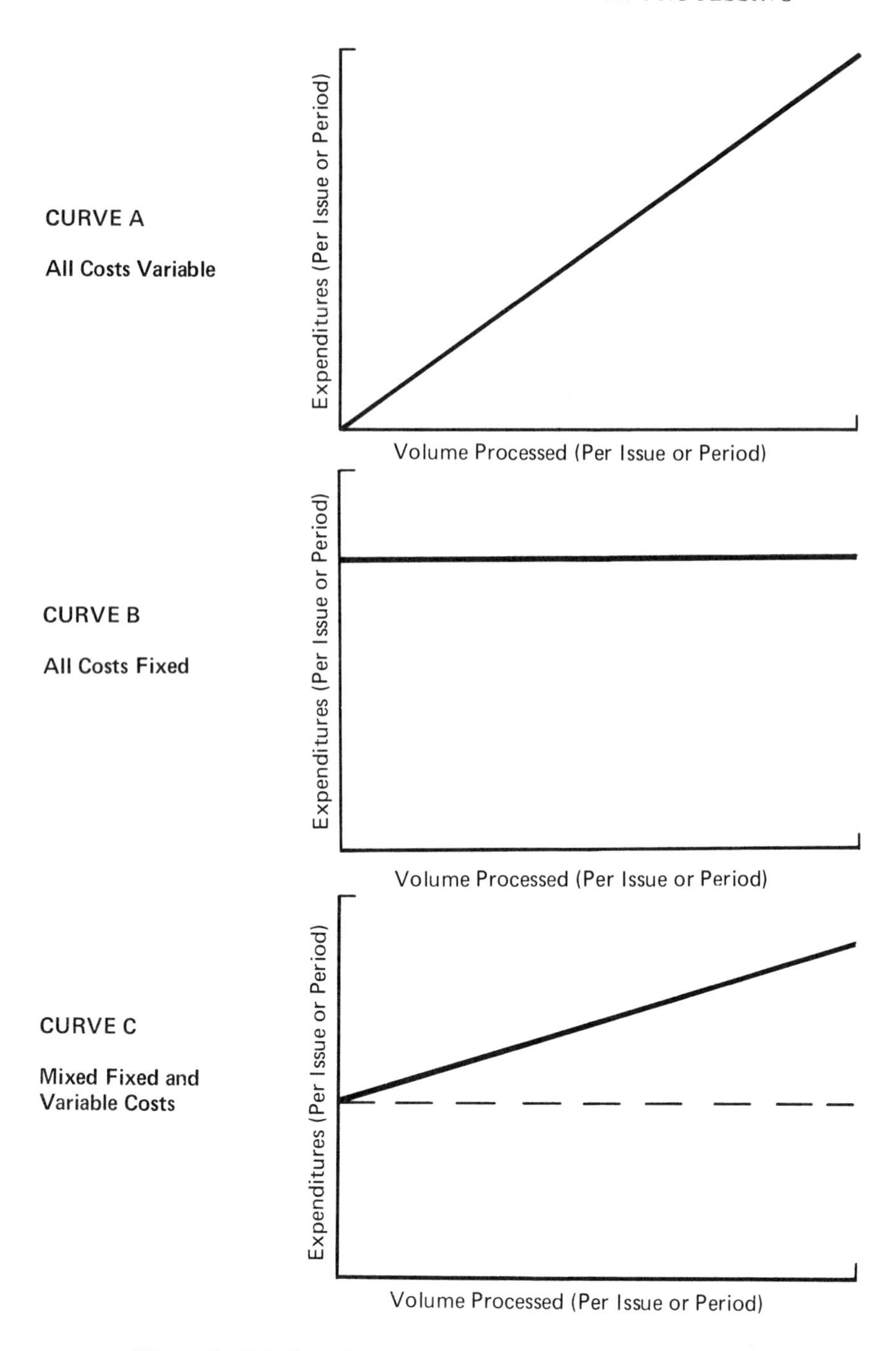

Figure 1. Relationship of costs to volume of material processed

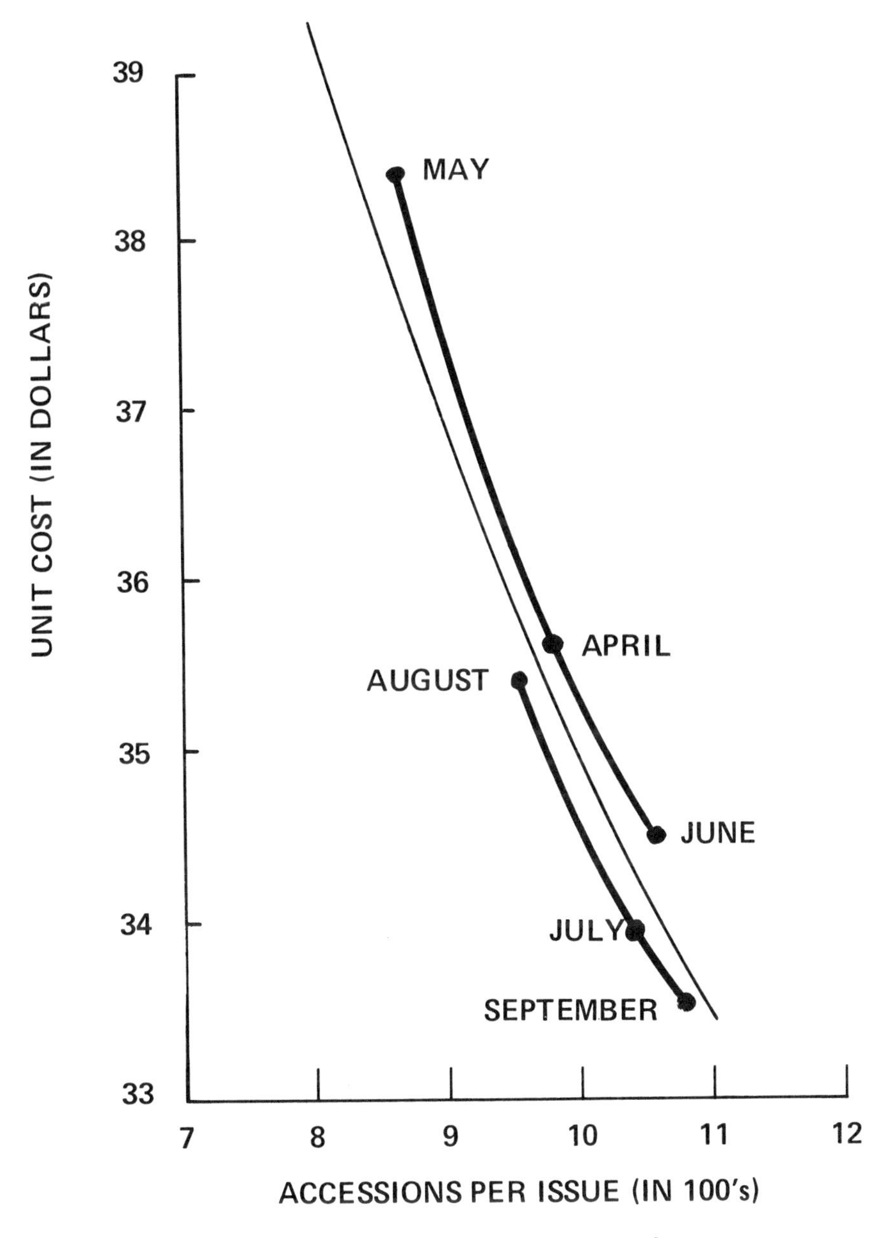

Figure 2. Variability of unit costs with volume

pose, it can be done. This is called "building block costing." Let me give a very simplified example of its application to an information system: the production of an abstract journal.

The typical gross unit cost for this might look like Figure 3. Obviously, this isn't very useful information, but suppose you could display something like Table 1? This table provides some useful information. Different things are measured by appropriate units; there are both unit and total costs; and the table shows where the money is going. Instead of taking heroic measures to cut the cost of abstracting and indexing, you might look at some of the other line entries and find pay dirt. Notice the print run of 5,000 copies with only 4,500 subscriptions. A cut in the overrun by 250 copies would give a result like Table 2. That's better than $1.25 off the average unit cost, without even touching the input processing. Let's look at the chain-printer index pages. The number of pages can certainly be cut by one-third by photocomposing them. This will give you something like Table 3—and look at those savings! Even deducting the cost of the programming, you are way ahead of the game in the first year, and you still haven't touched the input processing. Let's go one step further, and suppose that instead of this average figure per issue shown in the first column, you had the actual cost for each element of each issue and its volume, something like Table 4. The last three columns provide really useful information. By applying standard statistical analysis techniques, you can produce displays like Figure 4 (which should remind you of Curve C of Figure 1) and Figure 2, both of which were, in fact, derived from the numbers in Table 4. Here is information you can use for projections, evaluations, performance measurement, and a host of other things. It only takes a glance at Figure 2 to see that something happened between June and July which reduced the cost of subsequent issues.

Establishing a building block cost system which will give you this kind of information requires substantial preparations and careful—even scrupulous—execution. There are five basic components. I can only skim the surface of these components in this presentation, but details are available in two publications in particular. "The Cost of Information: A Prerequisite for Other Analyses"[2] provides a more detailed overview, and *Collecting and Reporting Real Costs of Information Systems*[3] specifies the requirements and includes many useful examples from real information systems.

Systems Analysis

The very first step in designing a cost system is a very detailed and very complete analysis of the operation you are going to cost. The usual activity of systems analysis, someone wandering around for a few days and then drawing pictures of the forest will not do the job for you. You will need a clear and accurate picture, not only of the forest, but of the trees, the

TOTAL COST $449,400

ACCESSIONS PROCESSED 12,000

UNIT COST $37.45

Figure 3. Excessively simple cost accounting

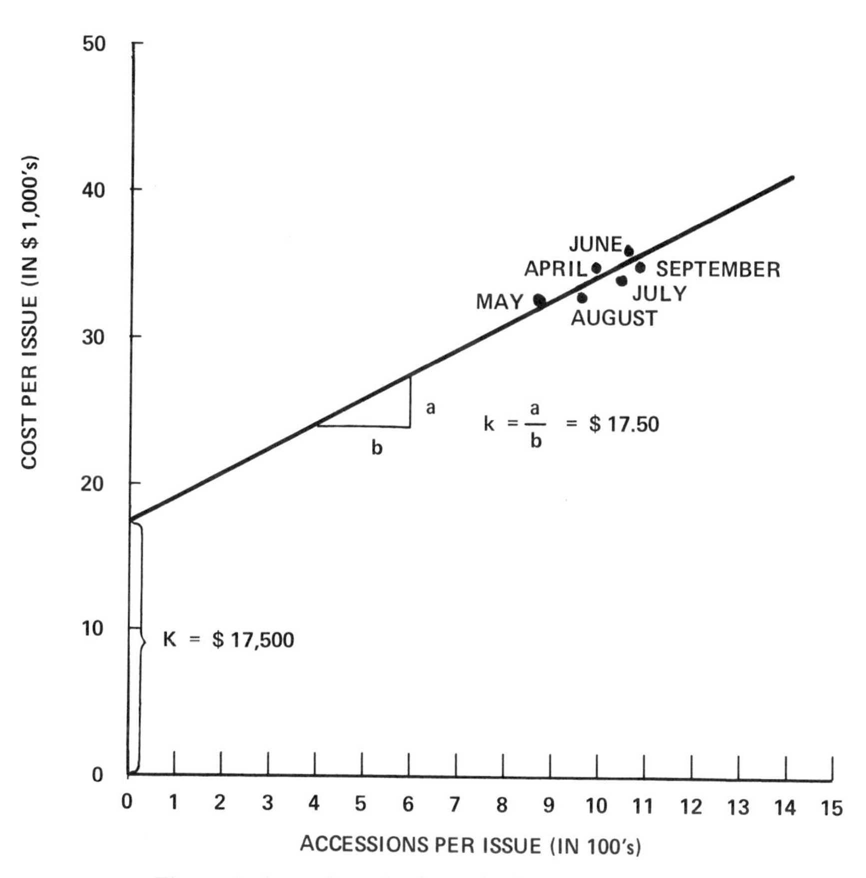

Figure 4. Journal production mixed costs by issue

	Per Issue	*Annual 12 Issues*
700 Accessions to file, with author abstracts @ $8.00	$ 5,600	$ 67,200
300 Accessions to file, in-house abstracts @ $15.00	4,500	54,000
150 Photocomposed pages @ $5.00	750	9,000
200 Chain printer pages @ $1.75	350	4,200
1,750,000 Pages reproduced (350 x 5,000 copies) @ $15.00 per 1,000	26,250	315,000
	$ 37,450	$ 449,400
With 4,500 paid subscriptions, annual cost per subscription =	$99.87	
Average cost per accession =	$37.45	

Table 1. Journal production cost for 5,000 copies printed

	Per Issue	*Annual 12 Issues*
700 Accessions to file, with author abstracts @ $8.00	5,600	67,200
300 Accessions to file, in-house abstracts @ $15.00	4,500	54,000
150 Photocomposed pages @ $5.00	750	9,000
200 Chain printer pages @ $1.75	350	4,200
1,662,500 Pages reproduced (350 x 4,750 copies) @ $15.00 per 1,000	24,938	299,256
Total	$ 36,138	$ 433,656
Savings over figure 4	$ 1,312	$ 15,744
With 4,500 paid subscriptions, annual cost per subscription =	$96.37	
Average cost per accession =	**$36.14**	

Table 2. Journal production cost for 4,750 copies printed

branches, twigs and leaves, as well. And it must picture the system as it actually is; not what it was *designed* to be or what it is *supposed* to be, but what it actually *is* now. The only way to get this is to dig in deeply at every operation, put the resulting flow chart on one piece of paper big enough to read, hang it on the wall (or lay it on the floor if you haven't the wall space), and invite everybody on the staff to examine, criticize and suggest corrections and modifications. Do not limit the invitation to professionals. Every technician and clerk should be given the opportunity to examine his involvement and see that it is accurately represented.

		Per Issue	*Annual 12 Issues*
700 Accessions to file, with author abstracts @ $8.00		5,600	67,200
300 Accessions to file, in-house abstracts @ $15.00		4,500	54,000
284 Photocomposed pages @ $5.00		1,420	17,040
1,349,000 Pages reproduced (284 x 4,750 copies) @ $15.00 per 1,000		20,235	242,820
	Total	$ 31,755	$ 381,060
	Savings over figure 5	4,383	52,596
	Less expenses		(25,000)
	Net saving 1st year		27,596

With 4,500 paid subscriptions, annual cost per subscription = $84.68
Average cost per accession = 31.76

Table 3. Journal production costs for index pages photocomposed

Product Number	*Description*	*Total Cost*	*General Allocation*	*Adjusted Cost*	*No. of Units*	*Unit Cost*
A03	March (Carryover)	$ 13,918	$ 332	$ 14,250	310	N/A
A04	April	34,046	1,054	35,100	985	$ 35.63
A05	May	32,060	5,920	32,980	860	38.35
A06	June	35,177	1,123	36,300	1050	34.57
A07	July	33,848	1,102	34,950	1030	33.93
A08	August	32,583	1,017	33,600	950	35.37
A09	September	34,705	1,145	35,850	1070	33.50
A10	October (Incomplete)	16,538	562	17,100	525	N/A
A99	General	7,255	(7,255)	—	—	—
Axx	*Totals*	*$ 240,130*	*$ -0-*	*$ 240,130*		

Table 4. Unit costs by issue

While you are building your flow chart, you should be trying to hang numbers on it. You will probably find that you don't have good figures for all the inputs and outputs for every block, but you should at least guess, just making sure that all inputs to any block are accounted for in the outputs. When you are through, you should have something like Figure 5. The details of this illustration are, of course, illegible, but it is only intended to show the pattern. Figure 6 is a segment of Figure 5 which is large enough to show the details. Note that all feedback loops and digressions are shown and that the inputs for both the whole and the individual blocks are balanced by the outputs. There are some external connections which are not shown to avoid confusion, but this is the sort of thing you should strive for.

The entire process of detailed, real-world systems analysis is a useful exercise in itself. I have never seen this done where it didn't turn up some surprises. Even if you never install a cost system, systems analysis can be a valuable management tool.

Identification of Costable, Countable Components

One might think that the ideal would be to count and unit cost every block in your flow chart. However, this is not so. Aside from the fact that nobody could afford to do that, there are many instances where the cost of collecting the data in such detail exceeds the value of the information derived. From Figure 6, for example, we developed only three unit costs: two order-fulfillment unit costs from the warehouse and by reproduction; and a request-processing unit cost which included all other activities shown. That was, in fact, an oversimplification, but we were under cost pressure and had to strive for a balance among what we wanted, what we needed and what we could afford, a trilemma with which I am sure you are all familiar. In any event, you have to be realistic about what you can get an accurate count on and how cleanly you can separate the costs associated with each activity. The fact that the same individual may be performing several functions does not necessarily mean that you cannot obtain separate unit costs for these functions, but you will encounter some situations where it is impractical and others where it is foolish to try. Some of these are discussed in the publications I mentioned earlier, along with techniques for identifying unit costable activities.

There is one point I want to bring to your attention here. In the course of analyzing several information systems, we have discovered a phenomenon which also applies, with modifications, to libraries. Figure 7 illustrates the division of information systems into five or six distinct categories. On the main line, we have streams of inputs directed at building and maintaining the data base in the center, and on the other side there are streams of outputs. The significant point here is that for the purposes of cost analysis, what comes out of the data base as outputs is totally different from what goes in as inputs. Not only do the elements of cost and the units of measure change, between inputs and outputs, they are almost independent of each other with respect to volume. The library parallel is obvious. If you transported the Chicago Public Library to the top of Mount McKinley, it might

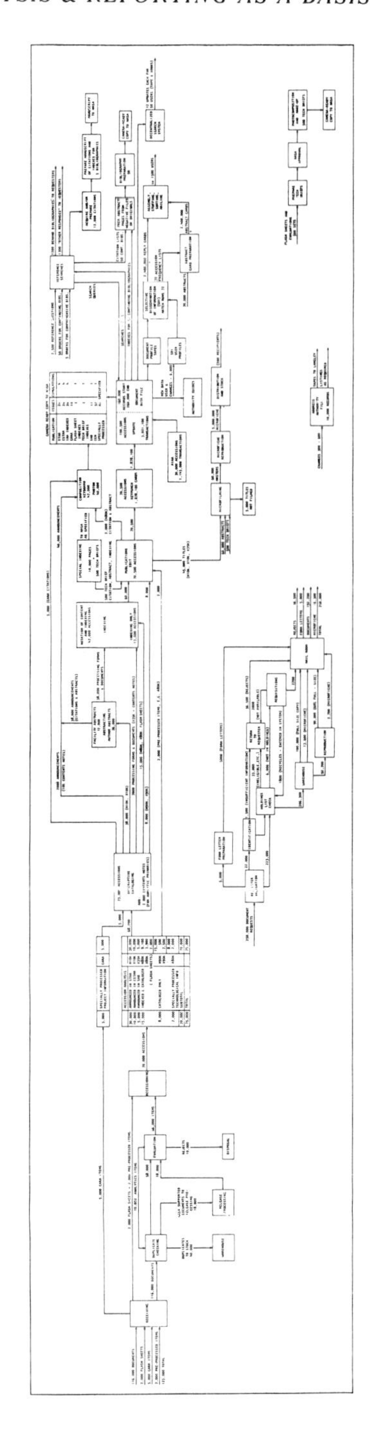

Figure 5. Materials balance chart (figure intended to show only scope of materials measured)

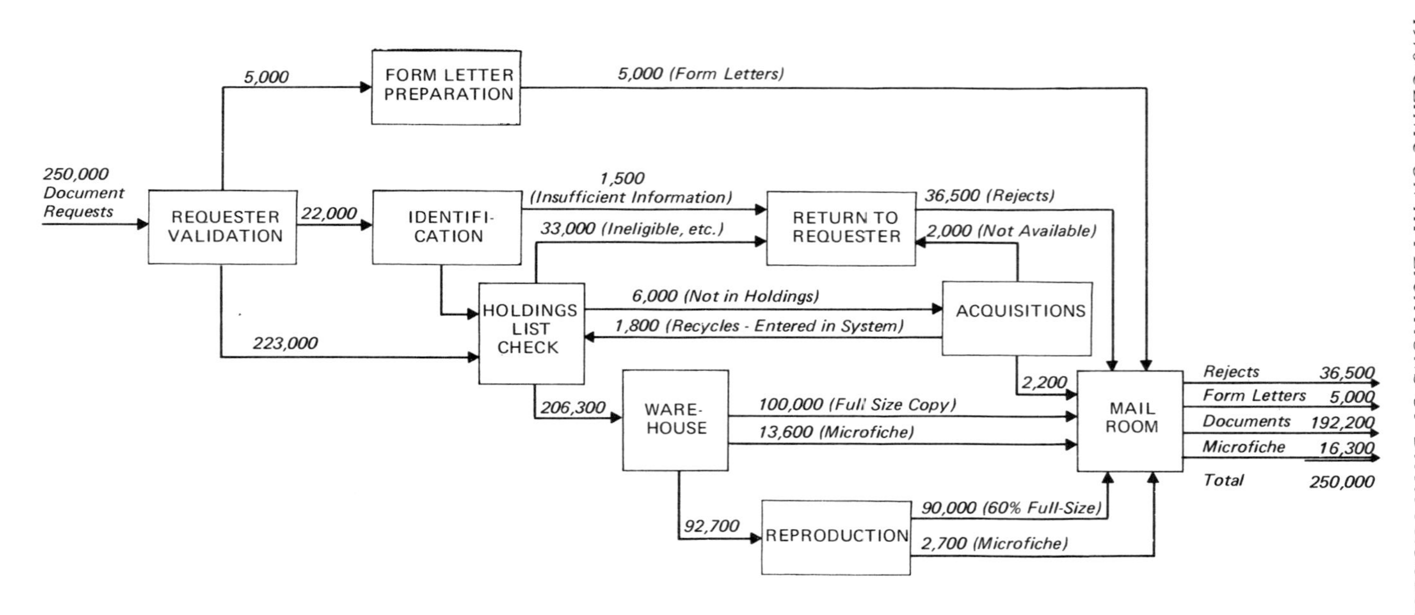

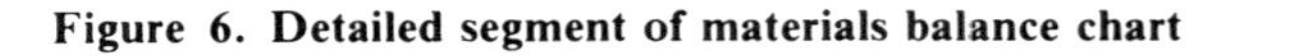
Figure 6. Detailed segment of materials balance chart

continue to acquire and process books and journals at its present volume, but its circulation and reference activity would drop to nearly zero immediately. On the other hand, if that library were to cut off all acquisition and processing today, reference and circulation would continue unabated for some time before they started dropping and would probably never cease entirely as long as the collection was accessible. Bear this separation in mind when you are analyzing your system. Touching on the other categories briefly: collateral activities are continuing activities which may draw upon the data base peripherally, but which require substantial additional resources (e.g., the document request activity displayed in Figure 6); ad hoc activities are one-time tasks and experiments, principally "emergency" assignments from the supervisor, which you will want to keep track of so you can at least answer the inevitable question about where the time went; administration and system development and maintenance may be either one or two categories, depending upon the circumstances, but they support each other and everything else.

Indirect Costs and Allocations

One of the knottiest problems of unit costing is the handling of the myriad costs which occur in any organization that cannot be directly associated with specific product lines. The approach most favored by accountants (because it is easiest) is to lump all of these indirect costs into one big pool and spread them across all product lines on the basis of some common cost element, such as direct labor (in which case, it is called "overhead") or total direct cost (in which case, it is called "General and Administrative," or G& A). The major problem with this approach is that it frequently swamps the direct costs. One organization provided an extreme example of this several years ago: for every dollar a client paid for direct labor, he paid $3.10 for overhead. A rate of 310 percent is high, but overheads of 100 percent are not uncommon. Another problem is inequity, e.g., inclusion of computer system development and maintenance in overhead when there are product lines which make little or no use of the computer. In library and information systems, there is the additional problem of what we call contributory products, where you have an activity which can and should be unit costed, but which is not an end in itself, and so must eventually be allocated to other product lines. The maintenance of a thesaurus or an authority file might be an example of this.

Basically, there are a number of different indirect costs which must be treated differently for useful cost analysis. The trick is to strive to allocate such costs only to the benefiting products and to do so on a rational basis. A fuller discussion of techniques of allocating indirect costs appears in "The Cost of Information: A Prerequisite for Other Analyses."[4]

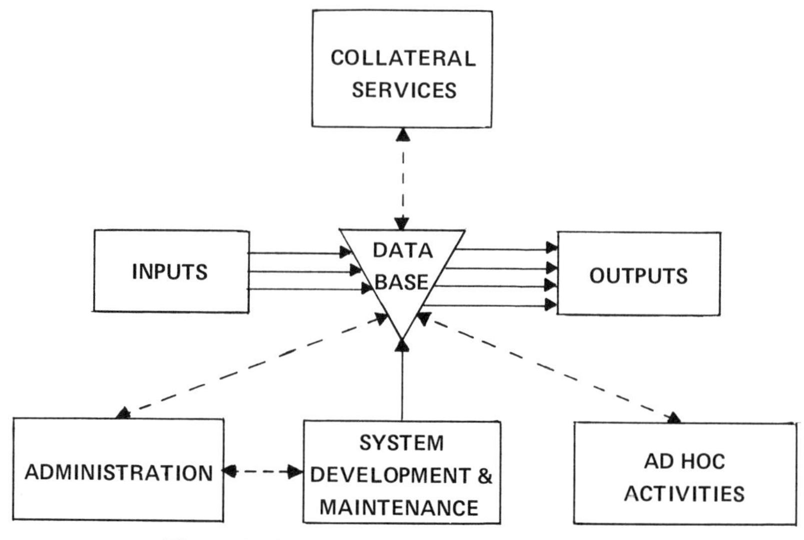

Figure 7. Overview of an information system

Collecting Cost and Production Data

After you have put together a cost structure to match your operating structure, you will be faced with the problem of collecting the data. You cannot simply tell your staff to keep track of their time and production; you must instruct them carefully and provide the tools which will make the task as easy as possible. These include: carefully designed forms for recording the information; handy, easy-to-use reference materials; mnemonic tags for the different products; and fast response to questions and errors. You must designate precisely what is to be counted, by whom, and how it is to be checked. Remember that for your unit costs to be valid, the production counts must be as carefully collected and audited as your costs. You must also bear in mind the necessity of relating specific groups of production units with the costs incurred in producing them. It is not always a matter of matching production recorded in a given period with the costs of that period; you have to contend with what industrial engineers call "float" or "dwell" time. It takes a finite amount of time for an item to undergo any process from input to completion. If that amount of time is a significant fraction of the period for which you are accounting, then a portion of the production recorded in that period will have been partially processed in the previous period and a portion of your production efforts in the current period will have been applied to items delivered in the next period. If you have very little variation in the volume or character of the work from period to period, you might be able to assume that one balances the other, but I have never encountered an information system where you could do this with everything. I doubt that you could do it in many libraries for technical processing, although you could probably ignore float time for book check-out. Encourage—nay, adjure—your staff to keep their time records current throughout each day. If they wait till the end of the day to make records, they will not be worth much. Remember also the learning curve. Don't expect to be able to use the first few months' data. Until the habit of current recording is firmly established, the data will be suspect.

Assembly and Rationalization

You can, however, use the early cost data for experimental input to your cost reports to insure that all the pieces will fit in their proper places and that everything will add up properly. The keystone of your system should be a report something like Figure 8. This is a summary covering an entire year and including the unit costs in a framework of total costs incurred. The detailed reports upon which this is based run to many pages, but the essence of building block costing is the fact that all of those details can be brought together to give you the total picture. Only in this way can you be assured of the completeness and soundness of your analyses.

THE USE OF COST DATA

It may seem that I have devoted inordinate attention to the construction of a cost system when the title of this paper implies that its subject is the use of cost data. However, unless the system for collecting the cost data is sound and the reports coherent, using them for decision-making is not only pointless, it is an invitation to disaster. Once you have a sound system, you really have a basis for making decisions. You have the capability to tell your board of trustees or the bursar precisely where last year's money went and a basis for justifying the increase you want this year. You will find the ad hoc activities records particularly valuable. It is surprising—sometimes appalling—how those "little" odd jobs add up over the course of the year. When you have unit costs and statistics for a year or two, you can construct your budget for next year with far more precision and confidence. You can also pad it more convincingly, if that is your inclination. When you are faced with a sudden cut in funds, you can more readily determine where to make the cuts for maximum savings with least impact on service. The costs and statistics are invaluable for monitoring your current performance against what was budgeted and for spotting trends before they become problems. If you make a change in procedure, you can readily determine its cost-effectiveness from information at hand. Look back at Figures 2 and 4. It is immediately apparent

	Prod. Class	Description	A Quantity Produced and Units (9)	B Direct Labor	C Fringe (2)	D Other Direct Costs Data Prep.	E Computer Services	F Printing and Duplic.	G Other (1)	H Subtotal Direct Costs	I Distributions (3 Management (4)	J Computer Operations (5)	K Other (6)
		Total Costs (1)		$250,000	$25,000	$25,000	$75,000	$50,000	$75,000	$500,000	$ -0-	$ -0-	$ -0-
GENERAL	Axx	Management and General		75,335	7,533			6,838	45,294	135,000	(135,000)		
GENERAL	Bxx	System Maintenance		15,000	1,500		12,500	200	3,650	32,850	12,150	5,000	
GENERAL	B10	Computer Operations		18,000	1,800			10	2,090	21,900	8,100	(30,000)	
SUPPORT	Lxx	Reference General		1,500	150				1,270	2,920	1,080		(4,000)
SUPPORT	L5x	Ref. Request Processing	18,000 Requests	9,000 0.5000	900 0.0500			180 0.0100	140 0.0078	10,220 0.5678	3,780 0.2100		4,000 0.2222
SUPPORT	D5x	Thesaurus Maintenance		1,800	180				210	2,190	810		(3,000)
SUPPORT	Dxx	Descriptors to File	700 Terms	2,800 4.0000	280 0.4000	1,575 2.2500	2,100 3.0000	7 0.0100	655 0.9357	7,417 10.5957	2,743 3.9186	840 1.2000	3,000 4.2857
SUPPORT	S50	Source Dir. Maintenance		1,800	180				210	2,190	810		(3,000)
SUPPORT	Sxx	Source Codes to File	2,100 Codes/Names	2,730 1.3000	273 0.1300	1,575 0.7500	2,100 1.0000	21 0.0100	718 0.3419	7,417 3.5319	2,743 1.3062	840 0.4000	3,000 1.4286
INPUTS	Pxx	Acquisitions Program		18,000	1,800			500	4,520	24,820	9,180		
INPUTS	Rxx	Report Resumes, ALL (ROx, R5x) (11)	20,000 Resumes	71,000 3.5500	7,100 0.3550	20,000 1.0000	25,000 1.2500	20 0.0010	980 0.0490	124,100 6.2050	45,900 2.2950	10,000 0.5000	
INPUTS	ROx	Report Resumes, Regular Only	15,000 Resumes	22,500 1.5000	2,250 0.1500	15,000 1.0000	25,000 1.6667	15 0.0010	935 0.0623	65,700 4.3800	24,300 1.6200	10,000 0.6667	
INPUTS	R5x	Report Resumes, Full Processing	5,000 Resumes	48,500 9.7000	4,850 0.9700	5,000 1.0000		5 0.0010	45 0.0090	58,400 11.6800	21,600 4.3200		
INPUTS	JOx	Journal Article Processing	12,000 Resumes	19,200 1.6000	1,920 0.1600			480 0.0400	1,760 0.1467	23,360 1.9467	8,640 0.7200		
INPUTS	Cxx	Acquisitions Data to File	30,000 Records	630 0.0210	63 0.0021	1,850 0.0617	1,350 0.0450	24 0.0008	69 0.0023	3,986 0.1329	1,474 0.0491	540 0.0180	
OUTPUTS	Yxx	Linotron Tapes (incl. CPC)	90 Tape Reels	45 0.5000	5 0.0556		3,150 35.0000		260 2.8889	3,460 38.4445	1,280 14.2222	1,260 14.0000	
OUTPUTS	Kxx	MDS Tapes (Contract Only)	600 Tape Reels	1,800 3.0000	180 0.3000		5,100 8.5000		191 0.3183	7,271 12.1183	2,689 4.4817	2,040 3.4000	
OUTPUTS	Txx Hxx	Computer Pages	39,000 Pages	390 0.0100	39 0.0001		13,650 0.3500		915 0.0235	14,994 0.3845	5,546 0.1422	5,460 0.1400	
OUTPUTS	Wxx	Photocomposed Pages	8,000 Pages	800 0.1000	80 0.0100		3,600 0.4500		6,149 0.7686	10,629 1.3286	3,931 0.4914	1,440 0.1800	
OUTPUTS	Uxx	Computer-Onto Microfilm Pages	9,000 Pages	90 0.0100	9 0.0010		2,700 0.3000		5,172 0.5747	7,971 0.8857	2,949 0.3276	1,080 0.1200	
OUTPUTS	Mxx Nxx	Pages Reproduced	1,800.000 1,000 Pages	1,800 1.0000	180 0.1000			41,400 23.0000	420 0.2333	43,800 24.3333	16,200 9.0000		
OUTPUTS	Gxx	Accessions to EDRS	20,000 Resumes	2,600 0.1300	260 0.0130			20 0.0010	40 0.0020	2,920 0.1460	1,080 0.0540		
SPECIALS	E99	Special Services		3,500	350			300	230	4,380	1,620		
SPECIALS	Exx	Manifold System Test		2,180	218		3,750		57	6,205	2,295	1,500	
SPECIALS													
SPECIALS													
SPECIALS													
SPECIALS													
SPECIALS													

EFF-5.1 (11/70)

L Subtotal Direct and Distrib.	M General and Admin. (7)	N Subtotal Direct and G&A	O Fee (8)	P Total Cost
$500,000	$150,000	$650,000	$100,000	$750,000
50,000	15,000	65,000	10,000	75,000
18,000	5,400	23,400	3,600	27,000
1.0000	0.3000	1.3000	0.2000	1.5000
14,000	4,200	18,200	2,800	21,000
20.0000	6.0000	26.0000	4.0000	30.0000
14,000	4,200	18,200	2,800	21,000
6.6667	2.0000	8.6667	1.3333	10.0000
34,000	10,200	44,200	6,800	51,000
180,000	54,000	234,000	36,000	270,000
9.0000	2.7000	11.7000	1.8000	13.5000
100,000	30,000	130,000	20,000	150,000
6.6667	2.0000	8.6667	1.3333	10.0000
80,000	24,000	104,000	16,000	120,000
16.0000	4.8000	20.8000	3.2000	24.0000
32,000	9,600	41,600	6,400	48,000
2.6667	0.8000	3.4667	0.5333	4.0000
6,000	1,800	7,800	1,200	9,000
0.2000	0.0600	0.2600	0.0400	0.3000
6,000	1,800	7,800	1,200	9,000
66.6667	20.0000	86.6667	13.3333	100.0000
12,000	3,600	15,600	2,400	18,000
20.0000	6.0000	26.0000	4.0000	30.0000
26,000	7,800	33,800	5,200	39,000
0.6667	0.2000	0.8667	0.1333	1.0000
16,000	4,800	20,800	3,200	24,000
2.0000	0.6000	2.6000	0.4000	3.0000
12,000	3,600	15,600	2,400	18,000
1.3333	0.4000	1.7333	0.2667	2.0000
60,000	18,000	78,000	12,000	90,000
33.3333	10.0000	43.3333	6.6667	50.0000
4,000	1,200	5,200	800	6,000
0.2000	0.0600	0.2600	0.0400	0.3000
6,000	1,800	7,800	1,200	9,000
10,000	3,000	13,000	2,000	15,000

LS&R

NOTES: SHEET

1. **Total Costs** – Total costs for all columns are the same as the Year-to-Date cost shown in the Expenditure Report for the corresponding period, except that Other (Column G) is the sum of the following line entries of the Expenditure Report.

Supplies	$ 10,000
Other Purchased Services	$ 15,000
Occupancy	$ 25,000
Other Miscellaneous Costs	$ 25,000
Total Other (Column G)	$ 75,000

2. **Fringe** – Fringe (Column C) is applied as a percentage of Direct Labor (Column B), and is shown at actual.

3. **Distributions** – The purpose of the Distributions (Columns I, J, and K) is to include in the total cost for a product a proportional share of costs which are either general in nature (not identifiable to a specific product) or which remain relatively constant regardless of volume. The negative entries (enclosed in parentheses) in each column zero out both the column and the line for which the cost is being distributed, since the distributed cost now appears as an added cost of the various product (s) to which it has been allocated. This prevents the distributed cost from being counted twice and keeps the Total Cost entries for the two Subtotal columns (Columns H and L) identical, even though the individual entries in each column are different.

4. **Management Distribution** – Management Distribution (Column I) allocates the cost of Director and staff, occupancy, etc. across all other products in proportion to the total direct costs as shown in Column H.

5. **Computer Operations Distribution** – This distribution (Column J) allocates the Systems and Programming costs attributable to Computer Operations (as opposed to systems design, programming, etc.) and Data Processing Materials costs across all products to which Computer Services are charged. This is allocated in proportion to the Computer Services (Column E) costs for each product.

6. **Other Distributions** – This distribution (Column K) is provided to permit transfer of costs for Reference General (Lxx), Thesaurus Maintenance (D2x, D5x), and Source Directory Maintenance (S50), which are "fixed" costs unrelated to volume processed, into the volume sensitive products immediately below, i.e. Reference Request Processing (L5x), Descriptors to File (Dxx), and Source Codes to File (Sxx), respectively. This separation of "fixed" and volume sensitive costs permits more accurate assessment of the impact of changes in volume, while the transfers allow the inclusion of all costs for the respective operations in a single total for each.

7. **General and Administrative** – G&A costs (Column M) are shown at actual.

8. **Fee** – Fee is shown at % of the subtotal of Direct Costs and G&A.

9. **Quantities** – Quantity Produced (Column A) figures are from the Year-to-Date column of the Weekly Report of Operations for the corresponding period. The Quantity Produced figure for Product 640 (Pages Reproduced) is shown as 1000's of Pages to provide more manageable unit costs.

10. **Unit Costs** – Where a line is divided into shaded and unshaded portions, the figures in the shaded portion are the Year-to-Date costs for the cost element and product and the unshaded portion are the unit costs which are obtained by dividing the dollars in the shaded portion by the number of units in the Quantity Produced & Units column (Column A) for that product. The unit cost is carried to four decimal places to permit display of unit costs which may be quite small for some cost elements of some products, and to simplify rounding. It is not to be considered an indication of accuracy.

11. **Report Resumes, ALL** – This line is a subtotal of the two following lines which distinguish respectively, between resumes for which the Facility is responsible only for editing and machine input, Regular (ROx), and those for which the Facility provides Full Processing, (R5x), i.e. cataloging, indexing, abstracting. These latter include QAD's, IBE input, acquisitioned documents not assigned to clearinghouses, etc. It should be noted that after the resume edit step, this material is mingled with other input for keying, computer update, printout edit, and Master Data Set update, so that the unit cost shown cannot reflect true total processing cost for these items. A more appropriate unit cost for these items would, therefore, be the Full Processing unit cost plus the Regular unit cost. This is not the unit cost shown the Report Resumes, ALL, but the sum of the two detail unit costs.

DEMONSTRATION COPY

THIS REPORT HAS BEEN PREPARED FOR DEMONSTRATION PURPOSES ONLY AND BEARS NO DIRECT RELATION TO ACTUAL COSTS OF THE ERIC FACILITY

Figure 8. ERIC facility unit cost report

that something happened between June and July which reduced the costs in subsequent periods. If you had made a change at that point, you would know that it had worked—or, if the numbers had gone the other way, that it hadn't. Incidentally, since the advent of the electronic calculator, displays like this have not been difficult to produce. There are several on the market which will do most of the work for you. I am certainly not a statistician, but it took me only five minutes with a calculator to produce the equations for those curves.

In short, valid, detailed unit cost data can provide a library director with the information he needs to be a manager rather than just the senior librarian. He can negotiate with the keepers of the purse strings from a sound footing and respond quantitatively, rather than qualitatively. If he has a Machiavellian bent, he can inundate them with numbers and charts to the point where they will give in to get relief.

CAVEATS

I would be remiss if I closed without leaving you a couple of warnings. The first is summarized in Figure 9. TANSTAAFL is an acronym for "There Ain't No Such Thing As A Free Lunch." A building block cost system is going to cost you money and probably more than your present method of cost accounting. Aside from the system analysis, design and start-up costs, there will be a continuing cost of processing the information to produce the reports and the not-inconsiderable cost in terms of lost productivity due to the time consumed in keeping the cost and production records. Everywhere I have seen it used, it has paid for itself many times over in better management, better control, better forecasting, and some actual cost savings, but you have to be willing to make the investment to earn the returns.

Another problem is the resistance of most people to change. It has been my experience that it takes extensive advance preparation to get the staff cooperation you need. Work hardest on the professional people. They tend to resist detailed time recording (perhaps because they are not used to it) far more than nonprofessionals.

The most common pitfall is assuming that mathematical analyses represent the real world; that they are gospel. Don't believe it. There are two traps here. The straight line in Figure 4 and the smooth curve in Figure 2 might lead you to assume that your real costs are going to change with the same smoothness over the full range of the chart. In the first place, as volume changes, at some point, you are going to have to hire or lay off a cataloger, or buy or dispose of a piece of equipment. Catalogers and equipment do not come in fractional increments; each is a quantum step, so your costs will take a quantum leap. In the second place, while the mathematical formulas make it possible to extend the lines indefinitely on the chart, they are actually valid only over a limited range. In Figure 4, for example, if the volumes started

TANSTAAFL

Figure 9. There Ain't No Such Thing As A Free Lunch

above the line, in response to Parkinson's Law, while if the volume increased above 1,200, the costs would either start falling below the line as you pushed your staff for more work, or put them on overtime, or they would jump up sharply if you hired an additional person.

The second trap lies in accepting a forecast as real just because it has been mathematically derived, even though it doesn't make sense. Take a look at Figure 10. If, in the last quarter of calendar year 1965, you wanted to project the volume of facility-prepared masters (the dotted line) for the next year or so, you could get two very different answers, depending on how much of the data you use. If you take only the last year's production, you will get a modest growth rate, but if you go back two years, you get a growth figure almost twice as large. On the surface, it would seem that the more data you use, the more reliable your forecast, but this is not always the case. The very fact that the 1965 growth was less than that in 1964 indicates that growth is slowing down. Mathematical projections are extremely valuable, but they are no substitute for professional judgment. When there is an apparent conflict, investigate to find out why, but in the last analysis, professional judgment should govern.

Figure 10 also illustrates another booby trap of forecasting. Remember that forecasting is an attempt to guess what is going to happen in the future using the best information available, but no matter how good your data or how careful your analysis, circumstances beyond your control can change to nullify your basic assumptions. In the case illustrated (which is real), the decision was made in mid-1965 to increase capacity to accommodate growth by installing a complete new production line with entirely new equipment using a new production technique. This was installed in the last quarter of 1965. Unfortunately, in December of that year, Uncle Sam issued the decree that, "Thou shalt not refilm a document which has already been filmed by another government agency." You can see what happened to the volume of facility-prepared masters, and you can imagine what happened to the unit costs.

LIBRARY COST ANALYSIS

In closing, I want to remind you that although building block costing was designed for information systems, the principles can—with appropriate modifications—be applied to libraries. When the system was first developed,

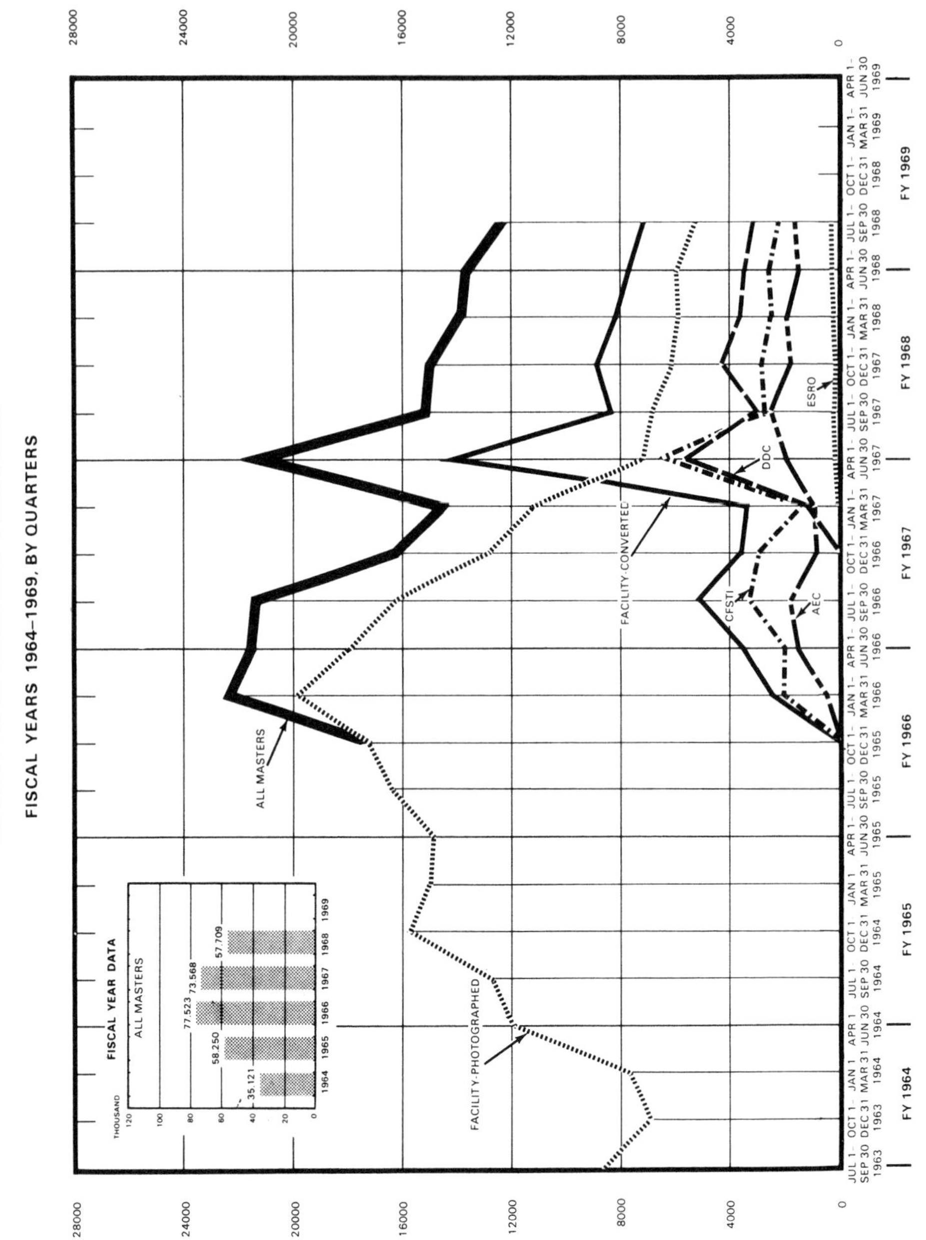

Figure 10. Microfiche master production

	Labor	Building Rental	Equipment Rental (Other than "Books")	Overhead Expenses	Total Costs
1. Acquisition	$ 2,482.06	$ 357.60	$ 42.00	$ 332.07	$ 3,213.73
2. Accessioning	1,440.08	331.20	36.00	194.86	2,002.14
3. Cataloging	10,179.50	1,535.20	228.00	1,381.93	13,324.63
4. Circulation	7,384.53	458.40	16.00	793.37	8,652.30
5. Public use of library (reading & reference)	2,626.82	25,615.50	3,086.00	511.15	31,839.47
6. Book storage	3,060.53	12,257.60	420.00	315.22	16,053.35
7. Periodical work	1,379.25	388.40	37.00	115.00	1,919.65
8. Binding	2,855.50	687.60	181.00	1,519.21	5,243.31
Totals	$31,408.27	$41,631.50	$4,046.00	$5,162.81	$82,248.58

Table 5. Summarized total of all operating costs
Source: Rider, Fremont. "Library Cost Accounting," *Library Quarterly* 6:376, Oct. 1936.

I was not so sure of this, but within a year of its first publication, my attention was called to an article in *Library Quarterly* by a professional librarian of considerable standing in the community, who had used almost precisely the same techniques in a study of library costs in a university. Table 5 is an illustration from that article. You can see the breakdown into coherent groups. All you need to do is divide by the units and you have something very much like Figure 8. If you read the article, you would have seen other similarities. If you don't remember seeing the article in *Library Quarterly*, it may be because it isn't very recent. It was written by Fremont Rider and appeared forty years ago, in the October 1936 issue.[5] How slow we are to accept new ideas!

REFERENCES

1. Bourne, Charles P. "Cost Analysis of Library Operations." 1971. (unpublished)

2. Price, Douglas S. "The Cost of Information: A Prerequisite for Other Analyses." *In* Robert S. Taylor, ed. *The Economics of Information Dissemination.* Syracuse, N.Y., Syracuse University Press, 1974.

3. ________. *Collecting and Reporting Real Costs of Information Systems.* Washington, D.C., American Society for Information Science, 1971. (ED 055 592)

4. ________, "The Cost of Information . . . ," *op. cit.*

5. Rider, Fremont. "Library Cost Accounting," *Library Quarterly* 6:331-81, Oct. 1936.

ADDITIONAL REFERENCES

Cooper, Michael D. "The Economics of Information," *Annual Review of Information Science and Technology* 8:5-40, 1973.

Olsen, Harold A. "The Economics of Information: Bibliography and Commentary on the Literature." *Information, Part II: Reports, Bibliographies* vol. 1, no. 2, March-April 1972.

Price, Douglas S. "Real Costs for Information Managers." *In* Frank Slater, ed. *Cost Reduction for Special Libraries and Information Centers.* Washington, D.C., American Society for Information Science, 1973, pp. 156-76.

________. "Rational Cost Information—Necessary and Obtainable," *Special Libraries* 65:49-57, Feb. 1974.

________. *Handbook of Costing for Information Systems.* Washington, D.C., Wiley Information Science. (In process.)

Wilson, John H., Jr. "Costs Budgeting and Economics of Information Processing," *Annual Review of Information Science and Technology* 7:39-67, 1972.

MAURICE J. FREEDMAN
Coordinator of Technical Services
The Branch Libraries
The New York Public Library
New York, New York

The Economics of Book Catalog Production

In the *Proceedings of the 1966 Clinic on Library Applications of Data Processing* appeared the article "Computer Applications to Book Catalogs and Library Systems." In that article, Donald Stromberg writes, "Advancements in technology will make [book catalog] service economical on a wide basis."[1] Today, I speak of the book catalog not as a tool of the future coming into being, but of its path to aphelion and its return to Coventry. Book catalogs were on the scene prior to the appearance of card catalogs, and we now see two major expressions of bibliographic information pushing the printed book catalog out of the important position it played in the 1960s and early 1970s. First, the book catalog-like medium, the microform catalog, is currently forcing the printed catalog out of libraries, and some observers are even predicting that the microform catalog, or, more precisely, the Computer Output Microfilm (COM) catalog, will completely replace the printed catalog within the next few years. Second, the on-line catalog as a tool for the library user (as distinct from the library staff) will have a heavy impact on the continued use of book catalogs as the on-line terminal is moved out of the back room and into the public service areas.

Put into a historical context, we see that printed book catalogs predated card catalogs,[2] were largely replaced by card catalogs in the twentieth century, returned in computer-produced form to replace card catalogs, and are likely to be replaced by COM and on-line catalogs for sound economic and technical reasons. The purpose of this paper will therefore be to explore this progression—book to card to book to COM catalog—and the factors which make the sequence a not-unreasonable one. The emphasis will be on the economics of the computerized book catalog.

Before proceeding, some caveats must be entered. There will be no specific costs given, such as "It costs $0.98 to produce a page of a book in photocomposed format, but $0.76 in line-printer multilith format." Detailed costs are meaningless without a specific context. For the same reason, I will not make detailed comparative cost analyses. If you are interested in these kinds of figures, commercial vendors will be glad to furnish quotations based on their price lists and your local requirements, and the literature already includes firsthand reports of costs in the production of printed book catalogs. Other speakers at this clinic will discuss the conversion of cataloging data to machine-readable form and the use and characteristics of nonprint output media. It is our hope that these papers will combine to provide a single, complex yet coherent whole.

THE DYNAMIC VARIABLES

Let us begin the analysis of book catalog costs by establishing the framework within which the book catalog occurs. Irrespective of format, the catalog performs at least two fundamental functions: (1) it organizes a storehouse of materials into a collection of materials, and (2) it provides access to these materials by identifying them in a variety of ways through some physical display medium. The following elements, which I will call "dynamic variables," apply to a functional definition and economic analysis of the catalog:

1. the size of the collection, and the frequency of changes (e.g., how much is added and weeded each year);
2. the rules for identifying and organizing the items, in the collection, and the number of access points to be provided to these items;
3. the media which are available for the physical display of the records expressing the contents of the collection;
4. the throughput function, i.e. the staff, equipment and production processes which are required and/or available for the creation of the artifacts through which the records will be displayed (or made available for display), including the number of sites at which the contents of the collection are to be displayed (i.e. in the central library, in branches, in every stack, etc.).

The costs of book catalog production, and the use and appropriateness of the automated book catalog, depend on these dynamic variables.

THE PRE-CARD CATALOG BOOK CATALOG

Prior to the ubiquity of the Ohio College Library Center (OCLC) card, and prior even to the universal use of Library of Congress (LC) cards, many libraries had typeset printed book catalogs. As the twentieth century approached, these catalogs began to fade into extinction, but they were important tools in nineteenth-century libraries. In terms of the dynamic variables listed earlier, there were several factors operative at the time. Collections were relatively small and stable; publishing output was low and new acquisitions were judiciously selected. The book catalog was economically attractive because the file of data it contained was not particularly dynamic; the technology for production had been well established; the book as a display medium had been acceptable for decades; and the short-title index type of listing found in many of the book catalogs of the day did not conflict with cataloging requirements because national standards had not yet been developed. (The original American Library Association cataloging rules did not appear until 1908.[3]) Furthermore, this situation was prior to the establishment of the interlibrary loan network, which developed in the twentieth century. If a patron needed a book held by another library, he or she had to travel to that library to use it. In effect, the printed book catalog served as the interlibrary loan device: library *B* would have a copy of library *A*'s catalog, and *B*'s user could, after consulting *A*'s catalog, go to library *A* to use the material desired.

The critical economic factors thus were: (1) printing was an infrequent cost because the library's collections were relatively static; (2) printing was (and is) a relatively cheap process for additional copies, although expensive for the first copy; and (3) the method of display in the old printed book catalog was up to the individual library, and for many the data were packed into line entries somewhat similar to today's telephone directories. Because there was no centralized source for standardized cataloging data toward the turn of the century, each library was on its own and did not have any significant economic incentive to go to a specific kind of physical display medium.

THE CARD CATALOG AND THE DECLINE OF THE BOOK CATALOG

Introduction of the Library of Congress catalog card service, coupled with more extensive collecting by libraries and the overwhelming costs of setting type for large and volatile book catalogs, served as the basis for the abandonment of the book catalog and its replacement by the card catalog in almost all of America's general libraries. Centrally disseminated standardized card sets removed a huge production burden from the nation's libraries. The letterpress book catalog was an inadequate medium compared to the cost-effective use of LC cards. Libraries around the country, regardless of past catalog media, found the card catalog irresistible. Let us examine the success of the card catalog in light of the dynamic variables suggested earlier. First, the twentieth century brought a wave of library growth as a result of increased publishing activity. Consequently, the catalog form had to be appropriate for the increased rates of change and growth. The letterpress book catalog was obviously uneconomical, because either new cumulations would have to be reset or noncumulative supplements—a burden to the user—would be necessary. The card catalog, on the other hand, allowed for instant updating and cumulation insofar as staff, card stock and (by this time) typewriters were available. (Actually, typewriters were a luxury for many libraries, as witnessed by the handwritten cards still to be found in many libraries.) If LC card sets were purchased, however, only filing would be necessary.

The increase in the number and size of libraries made it easier for library users to have their information needs satisfied at their own library. For this and the other reasons cited, the letterpress book catalog which was printed and made available to many libraries and private purchasers declined and was almost completely supplanted by LC-ALA rule-based card catalogs.

THE RETURN AND RISE OF THE BOOK CATALOG

The return of the book catalog was a two-stage process. First, under the brilliant and indefatigable leadership of its then-chief of the Card Division, John W. Cronin, LC published the first and greatest of its book catalogs, the *Library of Congress Catalog of Printed Cards.* Offset printing technology was applied to the problem of disseminating many copies of a whole catalog of data, as distinct from distributing cards for a single catalog record. The book catalog was now economically feasible because of improvements in offset technology. A 167-volume catalog representing the total of LC's collection for 1897-1941 was reproduced by photographing cards and producing offset page plates. Analyzing this book catalog in terms of the dynamic variables, we see the critical elements which changed. Typesetting was replaced by shingling and photo-offset—i.e. an expensive process was replaced by a relatively inexpensive process. Thousands of copies of this catalog have been sold to libraries all over the world. Its distribution in carload shipments to the same libraries is, of course, inconceivable in card form.

In light of the foregoing discussion, we can now make a generalization with respect to one of the dynamic variables. If there is to be a large number of sites for a given catalog, that catalog normally will not be in the form of cards. In the 1940s the photo-offset process enabled the book catalog to be established as a major solution to the multi-site location of cataloging data.

We turn now to the major topic of this paper: the computerized book catalog. We as users of the National Union Catalog (NUC) are aware that its reaccumulation will continue to be a problem for LC until all records are part of a machine-readable data base. COMARC (Cooperative MARC) is a project recently begun which is working on this problem. As a measure of this problem, searchers must look in four separate annual NUCs, three quarterlies, and three monthlies during the period immediately prior to the publication of a quinquennial. Economically speaking, this is a disaster for all concerned, including the staff who must reshingle all of the cards to produce each of the various cumulations, the most painful of which is the quinquennial.

It is now possible for the entire reaccumulation process to take place in the confines of the computer. Records can be reaccumulated by computer at any time, a gross departure from the laborious and expensive process of manual reaccumulation—the shingling of cards for offset printing.

Let us explore the changes which took place in the dynamic variables which had a direct bearing on the phoenix-like reemergence of the book catalog in the 1950s and 1960s. The major factor in this development is the key assistance of the computer.

At first, because of computer limitations, the book catalog could only be produced economically in non-research library dimensions. In other words, the size of research library collections and the rate of increase of holdings in the post-World War II period were both too great for existing computer technology. As recently as 1967 it was considered unfeasible to produce book catalogs containing more than 100,000 entries. How it became more feasible and less feasible in the course of a decade will be discussed further. However, many public library collections, especially the medium-sized systems and federations, were within the 100,000-title range in the 1960s.

THE ECONOMICS OF COMPUTER-BASED BOOK CATALOG PRODUCTION

As a result of changes in the dynamic variables, the computer-based book catalog became the ideal catalog representation for libraries as diverse as the University of California system, the research and branch libraries of the New York Public Library (NYPL), and countless smaller libraries.

The Size of the Collection and Its Frequency of Change

The size of the collection and the frequency of change prompted a turn toward the book catalog. The public libraries which received so much money from Library Services and Construction Act (LSCA) legislation during the 1960s found that reproduction and dissemination of cards neither met service goals nor was cost-effective. For example, a system which might buy twelve copies for twelve of its fifteen branches would have to create, arrange and file at least twelve identical sets of cards. Furthermore, users at the other three branches would have no catalog access to that particular title; these branches would not have cards for that title because they would not hold the book.

The system concept of libraries found a natural helper in the book catalog. By printing the entry and tracings for a title in the book catalog and indicating which branches held it, the need for the twelve sets of cards in the example was eliminated, as well as the costs of producing the cards and of arranging and filing them at twelve separate locations. Additionally, service was substantially improved because the patrons of the three branches, who formerly would have had no access to the book, could now use the system catalog and gain access to the total holdings of the system. Better service, i.e. access to the system's total collection, is purchased at a cost usually below the manual catalog costs for multi-branch libraries. This fact readily accounts for multi-branch institutions' change to the book catalog.

Computer technology made this type of catalog possible. The computer has the ability to take large files of data and reorganize them so that additions to those files can always be integrated or accumulated. LC's problem with NUC is that reaccumulation involves the manual reshingling of cards. Typically, the public library system with 60,000 titles would find it hopeless to reshuffle manually the approximately 160,000 cards for those entries in order to integrate the additional 16,000 cards representing one year's acquisition of 6,000 titles.

A significant development which occurred in computer technology was the passage from second-generation to third-generation equipment. Third-generation equipment altered the first dynamic variable—collection size and frequency of change—by making possible the creation of book catalogs of seemingly unlimited size. Because of this equipment, 100,000 titles ceased to be an upper limit to the size of a collection which could be represented by a book catalog. Computers of the IBM/360 class made it possible to store, manipulate and sort huge quantities of data within a time and cost framework which had not been practicable with second-generation equipment. Furthermore, advances in electronic photocomposition made possible the use of multiple type fonts and type sizes, thus permitting attractive and compact pages for the display of cataloging data.

The combination of these technological advances therefore enabled reaccumulation of large quantities of cataloging data in a timely and attractive fashion, and also enabled what was not practical previously: the inclusion of the holdings of all service outlets at every service outlet.

Some of the more conspicuous difficulties with the printed book catalog are: (1) the problem of what to do for patrons during periods between printings; (2) the significant time lag between the time the computer processes the data and the quantities of printed and bound book catalogs are returned from the printers (three weeks to several months, depending on the size of the catalog and the number of copies); and (3) the cost of the paper on which the catalog is printed. Even during the heyday of the printed book catalog, it seemed wasteful to discard outdated supplements and reacumulations. Present paper costs have exacerbated this problem.

Rules for Organization and Access Points

The second dynamic variable, i.e. the organization of the cataloging information and the access points, has not been greatly affected by the change from card to book catalog. The cataloging rules followed were the same and the number of access points was probably increased slightly. In divided book catalogs, certain entries appear which would not appear in a dictionary catalog, e.g., subject entries which duplicate title or author entries. The more complex issue which had to be addressed, however, was the arrangement of catalog entries. The computer is at its best and at its most ignorant in its literalness. Traditional filing in card catalogs involves exceptions and special routines for special entries. Even the abridged ALA filing rules is a book-length document.[4] It is virtually impossible, if not totally uneconomical, to try to get the computer to duplicate the traditional filing rules followed in manually maintained card catalogs. On the other hand, large catalogs organized by the IBM sort package would violate many important library cataloging principles, such as the disregard of initial articles for filing purposes; consequently, the adaptations are interesting. One library took the approach of creating filing forms for every entry. The net effect was, for example, the appearance of an entry in the catalog in the form "*1984*," but filed as if it were "Nineteen eighty-four" through the cataloger's input of the preferred filing form. (Computers can automatically create most of the filing forms, but for problems like *1984*, the cataloger must submit a substitute which overrides the computer-generated form.) This capability is one key element of the NYPL authority control system. The Library of Congress represents another point of view in its eighth edition of subject headings. Rather than manually constructing filing forms for the difficult cases or having the computer create them by comparisons of entries with elaborate tables, LC chose to simplify the rules to adhere more closely to IBM's filing routines. In LC practice, numbers are filed in small-to-large order, regardless of whether they represent quantities, dates or othr numeric information.

Other than by filing, the book catalog is not especially affected by the organization of data and the number of access points. It *is* easier and cheaper to add and change access points in a computer-generated book catalog than in a manually created and maintained card catalog. Unit cards have to be created, handled in some way to indicate access point, and filed—a great deal of work, and one of the reasons underlying the parsimony which runs throughout descriptive and subject cataloging practices. With book catalogs, authority changes are easy because the entire catalog is reprinted and whole files can be maintained automatically. This is virtually impossible with the card catalog except by using guide cards, an inelegant approach.

The Display Medium

The third dynamic variable identified was the display medium. Each display medium has its own unique strengths and weaknesses, some theoretical and others practical. For example, card catalogs are theoretically more up to date than book catalogs because the card catalog is continuously updated, while the book catalog is current only to the moment input ceased for the most recently printed volume(s). It is safe to assume that with a bimonthly printing process, the catalog is at least eleven to thirteen weeks out of date. In reality, one large research library was recently two years behind in filing subject cards, and many other libraries are regularly behind in filing. Although in principle the book catalog should be much less current than the card catalog, in practice it is frequently more current. More important, economic considerations make the outdated-ness of the book catalog acceptable because of the elimination of the time-consuming and expensive process of arranging, filing and revising cards for new titles. At libraries as large as LC, arranging and filing are actually separate, full-time jobs! Of course, computerized arrangement and printing in the book catalog eliminate these card-related functions and can result in substantial savings.

The cumulation process is a display problem, and as such is perhaps the most differently treated variable of book catalog production. In his article, "Optimization of Publication Schedules for an Automated Book Catalog," Michael Malinconico provides an analysis of and formulas for establishing publication schedules.[5] The drawback of the publication process mentioned earlier—that is, that volatile files regularly render expensive printed catalog supplements useless—creates a cost predicament which, at best, is a compromise optimized according to the Malinconico formulas. For example, the files of NYPL's branch system undergo continuous reaccumulation, a process which involves cumulation of all entries for one-sixth of the alphabet on a bimonthly basis, and a bimonthly cumulative supplement for everything not included in extant reaccumulations. Adding 35,000 titles per year, as the NYPL branch system does, necessitates this more elaborate process, with the result that every 2 months, more than 300 copies of 6 or more volumes become obsolete and are discarded.

For smaller collections, which have fewer additions, optimization is a seemingly simpler process. The individual library can weigh the cost and service elements of the publication process to determine a balance satisfactory for its unique circumstances. If 6,000 titles are added each year, it would seem extravagant to have monthly photocomposed and printed cumulative supplements, because there would be only 500 new titles added. For this reason, the juvenile catalog at NYPL follows a publication cycle totally different from the aforementioned branch adult catalog. The complete reaccumulation of the entries in the basic volumes and supplements should also involve the balancing of service and cost considerations. Many reaccumulate everything annually; others do so irregularly.

Assuming that the library has adequate financial resources, computer technology allows decisions about cumulation and supplementation to be wholly discretionary. Because of the costs and slowness of the printing process, however, the printed book catalog again faces diminution, and perhaps extinction, as a catalog display medium. The advent of COM and the letterpress-quality photocomposed microfilm soon to be implemented are factors which, in combination with the expense and slowness of the printing process, are prompting predictions of doom for the printed book catalog.

I would like to mention two problems with the computerized microform catalog which moderate any positive feelings I have about it. First, there is the capitalization of the microform equipment, a problem serious enough to have kept us from installing readers in NYPL's eighty-two branches. Although this is a one-time cost which can be amortized over a period of several years, it remains a significant problem. The second (and far more serious) problem is the state of the art of the display devices. There is no comparison between the quality of the printed page and that of the display of today's microform viewers. In all other respects, the microform catalog is superior to the book catalog.

If the book catalog is to maintain a level of service at least comparable to that of the card catalog, there must be sufficient copies of the book catalog to insure that the user has the same ease of access to the record in the book catalog as in the card catalog. We have regressed if the reader frequently must wait to use the desired volume of the catalog. Local analysis of the size of the card catalog and the number of users will determine the number of copies needed to replace the card catalog.

Before considering the costs of the elements comprising the actual book catalog itself (paper, binding, etc.), the quantity to be produced must be considered. Because the book catalog is reproducible, extra copies of the catalog can give net increases in the quality of service. For example, placing a copy of the catalog in locations such as bookstacks, circulation desks, community centers, schools, and dormitories brings the catalog to the library user, rather than requiring the user to go to the traditional single-site catalog. Requiring users to "go to the mountain" is at least an inconvenience, and an effective deterrent to use at worst. Additional copies provide better service for library staff, as well. Reference librarians, catalogers and other staff who have the catalog at their fingertips save the time of a walk to the catalog to find the information they need. The catalog is more likely to be used if it is near at hand, and may not be if its use requires extra time and effort.

Costs can be defrayed by selling copies of the catalog. Of course, the price of the volumes for sale must include overhead and all indirect costs of sales, as well as the actual cost of printing the added copies. I believe it is nearly impossible to recoup cataloging, conversion, and data processing costs (not to mention the research and development costs) through the sale of catalogs.

Other factors affecting the cost of printing entries in the book catalog are the decisions about where to truncate the data appearing with added entries and whether to print tracings with the main entry and/or added entries. Because we are no longer dealing with computerized catalog cards, these options are real. For cards, the duplication process usually involves some form of one-to-one copying of the unit entry by xerography, offset, etc. Given the fact that individual physical entries in a book catalog are constructed for each issue, one may choose—assuming the software permits—between the conflicting factors of increased printing costs and the added information which might benefit the catalog user. I have found that people who are experienced in the use of the card catalog want the full unit entry for each traced occurrence in the book catalog. I do not, however, know of any studies which actually have dealt with the need for full information. As a library user, I know that seeing all of the subject headings has often aided me in determining the utility of a given citation. Printing the tracings and truncating the added entries are two costs which can be controlled by the librarian.

Display costs are also affected by the density of entries on a page and the size of type used for printing. The use of photocomposed 6- and 7-point type will yield more data per page and offer greater legibility than the line-printer/offset output, which has no proportional spacing and only one size of type font.

Finally, the artifact itself has different variables. For example, the University of California Union Catalog Supplement (UCUCS) is an archival-quality printed and bound catalog. Nobody will soon be discarding the approximately 50 volumes which contain 750,000 entries. On the other hand, the variation in quality and stock for supplements to other catalogs is wide; I have seen mimeographed and staple-bound supplements. Many libraries find the best blend to be a plastic-impregnated paper cover (one brand name is Kivar) for the annual volumes, and a cheaper grade of paper, e.g., sulphite, for the supplements. Kivar is washable and largely resumes its shape when bent or wrinkled. A well-produced, perfect-bound, Kivar-covered volume will have all the endurance needed for even the most heavily used book catalogs, assuming that these volumes (unlike UCUCS) will be replaced after a year or two.

One further digression about sales might be noted in passing. The NYPL Research Libraries data base and book catalog system served as the basis for creating camera-ready copy for specific topical catalogs printed and sold by G.K. Hall. Usually a library cannot expect any significant income from the sale of its book catalog unless it is a national library.

The Throughput Process

As far as the economics of the book catalog is concerned, the throughput process is where the greatest variation in cost takes place. Gorman deals elsewhere in this volume with the cost of the conversion of the catalog record into machine-readable form and with the wide variety of methods and technologies available for that process.

In relation to the economics of book cataloging, it must be noted that the reason the conversion process is the most expensive (excepting, of course, the cataloger's labor) is that it is the most labor-intensive one. There must be keyboarding, and there usually is some kind of review, revision, or proofreading, depending on the method of conversion. Both hardware and people are required for this process, but these costs vary, depending again on the quantity and size of the records to be converted, the device used, and the degree of accuracy required. Some libraries contract out the conversion and computer processing, others do it all themselves, and still others have a mix of some work done in-house, and some outside the library.

Leaving aside the question of the quality of the labor and mistakes in design, software, and hardware selection, there remains a cost-quality relationship in the various kinds of catalogs. For example, a book catalog system such as NYPL's has in its design bibliographical or catalog control functions which usually are not found in other automated cataloging systems.[6] Of course, both software and data processing costs of such a system are increased because of the added computer files which must be maintained and the increased CPU time required for manipulating and comparing the data in these various files. It should be noted that some of these costs are offset by significant savings in labor-intensive areas of searching and cataloging.

In other systems, data processing costs can be held down by the use of simplified procedures, filing rules, etc. All of the cataloging is done off-line, and the computer becomes more or less a catalog-printing device with minimized bibliographical control functions.

In selecting and evaluating book catalog costs, one must find the mean which is satisfactory between these different values. One should bear in mind that better quality (or in a less judgmental way, greater elaboration of detail and flexibility of operation) almost always involves greater cost. Unfortunately, the converse does not hold true: great expenditures do not necessarily buy quality.

A SPECIFIC BOOK CATALOG PROJECT

The Hennepin County (Minnesota) Library (HCL), my former employer, has had an extensive automation program. I will review some of the specific cost-benefit strategies in the production of the HCL book catalog.

There were essentially three different elements affecting the economics of HCL's decision to convert to the book catalog from the card catalog:

1. HCL was growing rapidly; a projected ten to fifteen new branches were to be opened in a 20-year period, most of them during the earlier years.
2. HCL had a full-time systems analyst and a full-time programmer, as well as access to the county's more than adequate computer (originally two 360/40 models and presently a 370/158). Furthermore, HCL management shared the belief that a complex set of MARC-based bibliographical programs developed at one institution could be transferred to and used at Hennepin with a minimum of out-of-pocket research and development cost.
3. The Hennepin County and Library boards were committed to responsible management practices and were willing to make substantial investments in order to achieve long-range and, in effect, deferred savings.

It actually worked out as follows. Several samples were made of arranging, filing and revision costs in existing branches and for the first of the new branch catalogs being created. Overall, it was estimated that it cost a little more than five cents to arrange, file and revise each catalog card. On the basis of this, a projection was made of the estimated cost for creating catalogs for new branches and maintaining existing ones for the coming ten years. According to our analysis it would cost $100,000 more to start new card catalogs and maintain the existing ones than to convert the entire shelflist and all new records to the MARC format and subsequently produce book catalogs. The largest outlay was the one-time cost of retrospective conversion, especially because it was based on getting virtually clean records. This meant that every printout would be proofread and that no data would be automatically accepted.

With respect to the software transfer, details of the use of the UCUCS and NYPL software have been provided elsewhere. Omitted from the other accounts, however, was the fact that HCL, with its small data base in comparison to the combined NYPL catalog output, negotiated photocomposition, printing and binding costs identical to those received by NYPL and in effect based on NYPL's volume. This meant that in 1972, HCL paid approximately $0.70 per photocomposed page while catalogs for other libraries were being produced at prices ranging from three to six dollars per page—not unreasonable prices either. In terms of mistakes, the projected printing and binding costs were the worst estimates. Hardbound and sewn catalogs had been planned and the cost of them had been greatly underestimated. The final printing and binding charges for the Kivar perfect-bound, 5-volume set were just covered by the printing budget, and were covered because of NYPL's volume. Thanks to the printer's quality of binding, these softbound volumes provided the same or better service than the buckram ones would have. Because of their colorfulness and general appearance, I believe they seemed more approachable to the reader than a set of casebound tomes would have.

Some particular items which might be of interest regarding the planning and execution of the original Hennepin County Library book catalogs follow.

1. As with every automation project, almost all but the last date given was blown. Unlike many, *the initial cost estimates were not exceeded.*
2. Input costs were reduced by hiring keyboarders to work a second shift. This meant that fewer MTSTs, the conversion devices, had to be leased and that the output capacity was virtually doubled at no extra hardware cost. Library school students and graduates, all of whom had taken at least one cataloging course, were paid at intermediate clerk salaries to do the proofreading. Incidentally, the book catalog editing unit served as a valuable recruiting ground for HCL's professional openings and produced a quality of proofreading which would have been difficult to achieve with nonprofessionals. Conversion costs were further reduced and the quality increased by using the typists who regularly typed catalog cards and pockets. They were already familiar with the complexities of bibliographic records and did conversion keyboarding as part of their week's activity. One reason the typewriter MTST was selected was that typists, who are essentially trained to work with alphabetic data, would generally perform better than keypunchers who worked primarily with numeric data. The combination of these factors tended to hold down conversion costs for the particular strategy employed.
3. As to the display medium variable, we plunged. We printed 600 basic sets, 100 of which we over-optimistically thought we could sell. The branches were encouraged to have as many sets of the catalog as they thought they could reasonably use. It is interesting to note that photocopying of book catalog pages at the library's expense was encouraged to avoid ripped-out pages and to permit, in effect, the minibibliographies under some headings to be used in different contexts and not just to locate books in HCL's collection.

Overall library service was revolutionized at Hennepin. The reader at the smallest reading center was given catalog access to 1 million books and

100,000 titles; before that, he or she was only given cataloging information pertaining to 3,000 books. The most important change other than the creation of the comprehensive book catalog was the creation of a request/reserve/delivery system. A truck and driver went daily to the thirteen largest branches and searched their shelves for the previous day's reserves. At the end of the day, items found were delivered to the branch at which the reserve originated. Two staggering statistics emerged as a result of the change to the book catalog and the creation of the request/reserve/delivery system. The first change was that the number of reserves doubled each of the first two years—the result of giving catalog access to the total system's resources. Second, 75 percent of all of the reserves were found by the driver on his first trip, most of them being delivered to the branch of origin within forty-eight hours of the time the request was originally submitted!

In closing, we should understand that the prolonged existence of the current computerized book catalog is limited at best. Entire COM catalogs can be generated and duplicated overnight. Many libraries will find it less expensive to reaccumulate the whole catalog continuously rather than get into a main-catalog-plus-cumulative-supplement process. Microfilm and microfiche are trivially inexpensive in relationship to printed catalogs and the turnaround time for COM is incomparably faster. The cost and speed of computer-based microform catalogs will continually reduce the number of locally produced hard-copy book catalogs in existence in this country. And the primary factor is cost. My parting admonition, however, is not to confuse cost with quality—there is no necessary correlation between the two The printed book catalog is far superior to its alternative as an artifact to peruse, but it is certainly more expensive and is much more out of date. I would welcome a prediction from any futurologist about when and in what form the hard-copy book catalog will rise from its phoenix-cum-microform ashes.

REFERENCES

1. Stromberg, Donald H. "Computer Applications to Book Catalogs and Library Systems." *In* Herbert Goldhor, ed. *Proceedings of the 1966 Clinic on Library Applications of Data Processing*. Urbana, University of Illinois Graduate School of Library Science, 1966, p. 201.

2. *Ibid.*, p. 196.

3. American Library Association and (British) Library Association, comps. *Catalog Rules, Author and Title Entries.* American ed. Chicago, ALA, 1908.

4. Seely, Pauline, ed. *ALA Rules for Filing Catalog Cards*. 2d ed. Chicago, ALA, 1968.

5. Malinconico, Michael. "Optimization of Publication Schedules for an Automated Book Catalog," *The LARC Reports* 3:81-85, Fall 1970.

6. ———, and Rizzolo, James A. "The New York Public Library Catalog Subsystem," *Journal of Library Automation* 6:3-63, March 1973.

ADDITIONAL REFERENCE

For discussion of nineteenth-century book catalogs, *see* Ranz, James. *The Printed Book Catalogue in American Libraries: 1723-1900.* Chicago, ALA, 1964.

MICHAEL GORMAN
Head
Bibliographical Standards Office
The British Library
London, England

The Economics of Catalog Conversion

It will come as no surprise that, as an employee of a national library and one associated with the revision of Anglo-American Cataloging Rules (AACR), I did not agree with everything said by Mr. Kilgour in his opening paper. On one thing I am, however, in full agreement with him. I agree completely with his statement that the card catalog is dead. Many among us believe that it is dying, a few even believe that it is still alive and kicking. It is, however, as dead as a doornail. What I shall address in this paper is, in fact, the decent and economical disposal of the remains.

The title of this paper is as daunting to the person who must deliver it as it probably is to those who must listen to it. The topic of catalog conversion is a scattered one; it is something that has been carried out in recent years in a variety of different institutions and in a number of different ways. Major studies, such as the RECON and CONSER studies, have been made but no single method has emerged as the best and most economical. As a result, although the literature of the subject is extensive, the hard statistical and economic data contained within that literature are conflicting and, of course, are constantly being falsified by technological advancements on the one hand, and the ever-present inflation in the Western world on the other.

What I wish to do in this paper, therefore, is to sketch the processes involved in catalog conversion, and secondly to try to indicate the relative economic factors which apply to the various processes and strategies involved. I shall focus on one particular conversion project—carried out within the British Library—for which I had some responsibility, and I trust that this project will yield relevant information to librarians wishing to convert catalogs in the United States.

One of the most important aspects of the application of automation to library processing is the conversion of one's existing bibliographic files. In fact, a major constraint in many people's minds on the application of electronic data processing has been the query that it raises about the necessity for, and the problems of, conversion of existing files. I would like, first of all, to define what we mean by conversion. Conversion is the transfer of the bibliographic records of a library or group of libraries from manual to machine-readable form. This process can be enormously complex, expensive, and, in fact, daunting in its implications for the librarian and for the persons responsible for the establishment of an automated library system. The chief cause of the anxiety which many people feel about library catalog conversion is the expense of the process. For example, in 1970, John Jolliffe estimated that the conversion of the British Museum catalog to machine-readable form would cost £750,000.[1] In the intervening years, that figure has almost certainly doubled. This means that the cost of converting what is admittedly one of the world's largest and finest catalogs is now something in excess of $3,500,000. Similar figures would undoubtedly apply to the conversion of any similarly large bibliographic files.

The first task that arises, therefore, is to examine the benefits that one might hope to achieve from the expenditure of such a considerable sum of money. There are, broadly speaking, two benefits. The first is the fact that a converted file will provide the original data base for one's automated library system, to which can be added records derived from current cataloging and processing, or from centrally provided machine records, with the aim of providing an integrated file. The second benefit is the indisputable fact that machine-readable systems provide a better service to the users of the library than do manual systems. Even in these economically difficult times, it is thus possible to argue that one should endeavor to have one's existing files converted to machine-readable form.

Two fundamental points about catalog conversion shoud be noted before examining the details of the process. The first is that the most economical way of carrying out the process of catalog conversion will be to base it on the prior conversion of extensive regional, national and international files, and the widespread availability of records from these files. In other words, it is economic lunacy for every library to embark on its own individual, independent, and self-financed conversion program. Why is this? The answer lies in the simple fact that if one were to convert, let us say, the files of the two or three largest libraries in the English-speaking countries, one would have a reservoir of converted records which would account for a very high percentage of the items held by individual libraries within those countries. The conversion process would therefore not be replicated in a potentially nonstandard way, but would be done once in a standard way which would provide high quality machine-readable records, at a much lower cost than a library could achieve by developing its own conversion process. For example, the back files of the British National Bibliography (BNB) (some 400,000 records relating to British monograph publications since 1950) have been converted to machine-readable form and are to be made available to libraries wishing to establish machine-readable catalogs. In Britain, the authorities or bodies responsible for local public libraries, have been amalgamated and reorganized to form fewer and larger library systems. Some estimates of the percentage of the holdings of libraries covered by the BNB-converted file and another linked project are as high as 90 percent.[2] I will return to this project later, but wish now to establish the fact that this relatively small conversion operation (costing approximately £75,000 or $150,000) has made possible the distribution of MARC-compatible records at a much lower unit cost than would have been the case had these libraries started their own conversion projects. In fact, independent conversion may be simply impossible for many library systems which lack the economic and human resources required for such a project.

The second fundamental point is that before conversion of one's file is begun, using the maximum number of externally available previously converted records, one should establish a current automated cataloging and processing system. I believe it is very poor strategy to try to establish a current processing system and to carry out the conversion at the same time—or to attempt to begin the conversion without a complete definition of the current system—its structure, methods and aims. To begin a conversion project before the current processing system is operating will have at least two bad consequences: (1) converted records will run the risk of being unsuitable for the finally developed current system, and (2) the conversion project will absorb some of the financial and human resources which should be concentrated on the current system.

The various aspects of the conversion process involve: (1) the selection of data to be converted, (2) the coding of that data to make it acceptable to the machine system, and (3) the transfer of the coded data from human-readable to machine-readable form. Consider first the selection of data. A primary objective should be to establish for which items held by your library records are already available in machine-readable form. For libraries in the United States there are two main sources for these records: (1) the existing MARC data base built up by the Library of Congress, and (2) the data bases which have evolved from the establishment of cooperative systems and networks. For example, the OCLC system is capable of providing records for a large number of more recent publications, and the CONSER project will provide records for more than 250,000 serial publications. The unit cost of a MARC record supplied by the British Library is twenty cents. Comparative figures for the independent production of records are notoriously difficult to obtain and interpret, but in most circumstances the unit cost to the library will be much higher. Furthermore, such a simple cash comparison does not take into account either the standard of the centrally obtained record (as compared to the locally produced one), or the staff hours involved in complete local production. The use of these externally provided records will, of course, dictate one of the standards necessary to establish for a conversion project, that is, the format in which the records will be received will be the MARC format or at least will be in a MARC-compatible format.

It is, of course possible to convert a MARC record into a nonstandard format, and there may in some instances seem to be advantages for an individual library in constructing a format which is of particular use to them. Nevertheless, I would strongly urge that all conversion projects and, by implication, the ongoing cataloging and processing automated systems, be based on the use of standard formats. I would urge this for one very simple reason: any automatic transfer from one format to another can at best only *maintain* the level of analysis and definition contained within the format from which one is converting, and more often involves a loss of definition and analysis. One can always create less out of more but can rarely create more out of less. Therefore, the evolving bibliographic order will demand, as seems inevitable, the use of a standard format for the exchange of records and, one would hope, for the use of records within local, regional, national, and international systems. There must be a mechanism for determining which items in one's library have externally produced records available. Ideally, this would be by a standard numbering system, such as identifying the Library of Congress card number or the International Standard Book Number for an item; if such numbers are not available, a search strategy will have to be evolved, depending almost certainly on the author and title of the work. These access points are difficult to determine and use in a fully standard way, and it will therefore be necessary to address the problem of identifying a record and establishing its identity with the item in one's library. Various strategies have been advanced in connection with the MARC/RECON project,[3] and it seems likely that the strategies established by the OCLC network users will be of great significance for libraries wishing to assess records which are outside the commonly used numbering systems.

We now come to the consideration of the conversion of entries relating to those items for which no externally produced records are available. As stated above, the question of the format in which these records will be created has been settled. That is, it should be an agreed basis for the conversion program that records be created in the MARC format. Other standards, however, are not as immediately apparent. Does one attempt to transfer all information held in one's current catalog? Does one attempt to change that information to ensure that it conforms to currently accepted national and international standards? To answer the first question, it is not necessary for the library to convert all the information which is held. It might be desirable, in an abstract way, that our future machine systems hold very full bibliographic information, and this is recommended in the report of the RECON pilot project.[4] However, practicality and economics seem to dictate that it will be necessary in many cases to establish a *minimum* set of data for the items held in one's library, and that the criteria for the establishment of this minimum set of data should be: (1) which elements provide the most important access to the whole record, and (2) which elements are necessary for the identification and adequate description of an item. The traditional catalog entry has been a very full one. To some extent, it harks back to a previous era of bibliographic description and contains much information which many would regard as not germane to the purpose of a modern local library catalog, even those catalogs which represent very large collections. I would like to suggest a minimum set of data to be included in all converted records:

1. the class number and/or call number,
2. the various author headings,
3. the subject heading(s),
4. the uniform (filing) title (if present),
5. the title proper (as defined by the ISBD(M)),
6. the edition statement,
7. the publisher and date,
8. a truncated form of the physical description of the item, and
9. a short series statement.

These elements will, I believe, provide enough information to access the record and will adequately describe it to the user once the record has been found.

By this stage in the conversion process, one has identified the items for which externally produced records can be obtained, and has decided on a set of data to be recorded for the items to be converted locally. The next stage is to edit and code the entries in the manually produced catalog for their transference to machine-readable form. A full set of information must be used for this purpose. In most North American libraries the most suitable entry is the shelflist entry because this gives not only the descriptive details, heading and call number, but also the other headings for the item being described. This is necessary because a machine-readable record is more extensive than any one catalog entry. It is worthwhile to point out also that the use of the shelflist is frequently less disruptive of ordinary catalog use than is the use of other catalog entries.

Once the shelflist entries for the items to be converted have been identified, the next process is to code the information. This can be done in a variety of ways, and I will now describe and comment on the way in which this process was carried out for the BNB-conversion mentioned earlier. The basic entries were given to a group of persons consisting of professional librarians and library school students, to be edited on a "cottage industry" basis and according to a strictly prescribed set of rules. These rules were: (1) to select those entries which fell within the scope of the project (for example, repetitive entries for continuations were excluded), (2) to cross out from the entry any element not considered to be relevant in the conversion process, and (3) to add distinctive punctuation and numerical and alphabetic coding to indicate the class of information to be converted. In this application, "cottage industry" means that the people did this work at home at a fixed price for a certain number of entries. At that time it was £2.00 (about $5.00 in those days) for 100 entries—though it would now be more. The advantage of the system is a rather simple—and to a certain extent brutal—financial advantage: work done at home is not subject to "overheads." In his study of the costs of conversion of bibliographic records to machine-readable form, Duchesne established that in 1971 the overheads were equivalent to 100 percent of salary paid, and it is unlikely that in the intervening years this percentage has decreased.[5] In other words, to organize work in a factory, library, etc., will cost more than $2.00 in real costs for every $1.00 of salary paid. The advantages, therefore, for the library and for the persons thus temporarily employed are, I think, obvious.

So far as the coding is concerned it is sufficient to say that enough information was added to the records to produce a MARC-compatible record. For example, a simple numerical code was added by the side of the heading to indicate the class of personal or corporate heading to which it belonged. It was not necessary to code the heading further, because in a sophisticated and homogeneous file like BNB the same typographic conventions had been used over the years so that, for instance, once one has coded a heading as being a personal name, an element in roman type preceded by a comma must be a forename, and an element in italic type preceded by a comma must be an epithet. Thus, an element of automatic format recognition (AFR) can be combined with the precoded information, even in situations where complete use of that technique is not possible. This combination of partial pretagging and AFR was also used in the RECON pilot project.[6] In the rest of the entry, each element was separated from the next by a standard punctuation mark. This particular coding exercise was done directly onto photocopies of the printed BNB entries. It would be possible, of course, to photocopy cards directly from a shelflist card catalog. Another method would be to devise a standard worksheet with precoded pigeonholes or boxes; professional transcribers would then fill in this sheet from the evidence provided by the entries. This latter course has several disadvantages in that it involves paying professional staff to write or type data, the possibility of transcription error is increased, and it takes longer. For these reasons I would suggest that the coding of existing data is more economical. At this point one shoud question whether professional (or trainee professional) work is required for coding. In our experience it is necessary, partly because the coding or the transference of entries to a worksheet is not an automatic or a clerical process, and partly because it may be necessary (and in the case of a catalog which has been built up over a period of time and which has a considerable history, it *will* be necessary) to amend the bibliographic information before its transference. For example, the BNB entries reflected for most of their history the 1908 cataloging rules and the converted entries were intended to form part of a data base which was based on the 1967 cataloging rules. It was necessary to decide for example, the relevancy of certain elements of personal headings, and the form of many corporate headings. These decisions cannot be made by clerical staff without a considerable amount of training. Experiments we did using nonprofessional staff for coding and amendment indicated that the amount of error created by lack of knowledge of cataloging rules was unacceptably high; these errors had to be corrected at the proofreading stage, which is even more expensive than the stage of the creation of the coded data. This amendment of bibliographic data is necessarily limited. The form of the bibliographic entry can be changed, but such matters as the different choice of main entry by different cataloging rules, and the changes in class numbers necessitated by different editions of (say) the Dewey Decimal Classification, cannot be done exactly without reference to the actual item itself. It is an axiom of catalog conversion that the only economical way to carry it out is by using the data already present in the system. Any attempt to recatalog or reclassify the actual items will prove to be ruinously expensive.

One other problem remains at this stage of dealing with any file—the identification of duplicate records. These duplicate records either refer to different copies of the same item or to items which are too similar to require separate description in the converted file. I will mention here two ways of identifying duplicates. Call numbers, if they have been consistently applied, can be matched and will provide a list of suspect duplicates should the same call number occur on more than one record. Another possible strategy is the matching of certain data fields. A coincidence of title proper and date will provide a list of almost certain duplicates. A more interesting and advanced technique is that which was developed by the Project LOC[7] which was devoted to records relating to early printed books. This is the technique known as "fingerprinting." The theory behind fingerprinting is that it provides a unique identifier for an issue of a book by taking certain arbitrary data. To take an imaginary example, these might be the first four letters of the title proper, the first three letters of the publisher's or printer's name, and the first and last three letters on page twelve. It has been demonstrated that such assemblages of data provide a very high degree of accuracy in identifying duplicates even in old established catalogs where items have been acquired over a great many years and where the descriptive cataloging practices have varied a great deal over those years. The fingerprint also provides a control "number" for the converted record. In the absence of an ISBN, LC card number, or other unique identifier, it is necessary to devise a control number system. The only criterion upon which this should be based is that the number should be compatible (of the same length and type) with the control numbers used for records in the established or projected current cataloging system.

The next stage in the conversion process is the transference of the coded information into a form which can be fed into the computer system. In the BNB system to which I have been referring, the coded and edited data were keyboarded by persons who not only were not professional librarians, but also were not familiar with the content and structure of bibliographic records. This was possible because the BNB entries were printed, and therefore the basic information on them was of a high level of legibility, and also because the simple coding and punctuation conventions meant that data could easily be transcribed by persons who were unfamiliar with library techniques. Once the records were keyboarded in the coded form they were very simply converted by program into MARC format. This process did, of course, not create complete MARC records, but did create records that were within the parameters of the holding MARC format standard (ISO 2709) and hence were compatible with existing UK MARC records.

In this system the keyboarders were linked via a minicomputer to a CRT display, on which they could see the records which they were keyboarding. There were very simple amendment and error-correction techniques. Among these were certain automatic validations; for example, certain fields and elements (e.g., the title and date) were mandatory, and if they were omitted a signal was shown on the screen. The program also supplied an automatic series of tags in the normal sequence. This reduced keyboarding costs by eliminating the necessity for keyboarding the tags, and also helped to eliminate error by presenting the keyboarder with the logical next element. Rejection of an element thus became a conscious decision (because an element of data was not present in a record) rather than an unconscious error. The costs of keyboarding data are analyzed by Duchesne,[8] and inflation and increased labor costs have combined to increase these figures considerably. A reasonable current estimate is sixty pence (approximately $1.20) for one thousand key depressions. Any strategy which reduces the number of key depressions is, therefore, of great value. To take a simple example, the decision to supply the period after the third digit of a DC number by program, rather than keyboarding it, saved more than one-half million key depressions in the BNB conversion. Other punctuation, subfield codes and capital letters can also be supplied by program.

The method used for keyboarding data in the BNB conversion is, of course, only one of a great many ways of submitting the data to the computer system. Other significant methods include the punching of paper tape or cards, the preparation of magnetic tape for batch processing, and the presentation of data directly on-line to the data base. Another method other than straightforward keyboarding which has been widely discussed is that of optical character recognition (OCR). This technique depends on the creation of cataloging data in a special typeface in which the letters, numbers, and symbols are sufficiently individualized to be read by electronic scanners and automatically transferred into machine-readable form. Investigations into using OCR techniques on conventional typefaces or conventional typewritten characters have been carried out. It seems unlikely, however, that in dealing with the catalogs which we have at present, with their inconsistencies in type and presentation, that such techniques can be used directly. In other words, there will have to be in the use of OCR techniques, for the foreseeable future at least, an intermediary stage of transference from conventional letterpress or typewritten characters into electronically readable characters. The most economical method for the future is likely to be the direct interaction, using on-line techniques, of the keyboarder and the data. That is, records will be immediately processed and presented on a CRT to the keyboarder or keyboarder/editor so that the information can be seen to be correct as it is added to the file. Recent advances in technology have made this method both feasible and likely to be economical.

The next stage in the conversion process is the checking of the data by the professional staff—the "proofreading" process. It is clear that to put the maximum amount of professional effort into the coding and editing of the data before keyboarding will save on proofreading and amendment costs. These costs are likely to be rather high for two reasons. One is that the proofreading activity—the activity of editing the file—is something that must be carried out by high-level professional staff. It cannot be reduced to a clerical routine, nor can it be entrusted to relatively inexperienced professional staff thus making per hour costs high in the proofreading stage. Additionally, the amendment process generally requires substantially more in computer resources per record than does the creation process. For these reasons correction of errors at the proofreading stage is expensive and time consuming. Another reason for the expense is that amendment costs are also high; either the file must be accessed to put in replacement fields (or in extreme instances, whole replacement records), or the records must be called on-line so that they can be checked and amended. Either way this is an expensive and time-consuming process. A certain amount of proofreading and amendment will be necessary even when the input is of high quality, because catalogs and bibliographic files are complex structures. They are more than a heap of glittering baubles—a mere assemblage of records; they are systems which allow the user to relate one record to another, to establish the identity or nonidentity of two or more items, and to survey groups of records sharing a common characteristic. Therefore, an overview is needed. We took the view in the BNB conversion process that a sample proofreading technique would be adequate. This was because we had devoted a considerable amount of time to high-quality editing at input, and also because the entries from which the input was taken were similar in quality and level of bibliographic standardization. Even with such a situation, however, we found that a sample proofreading of one item in every ten (paid for at a rate double that of the editing rate) did not result in satisfactory quality control. It seems to be necessary to maximize the quality of input and to supervise that quality very closely, but also to make sure that there are resources available to ensure a complete overview of the results of the conversion process.

One important general question which arises in considering the conversion of bibliographic files is that of training staff for editing, keyboarding, and proofreading. Undoubtedly the best staff for a conversion project consists of those who are familiar with the creation of records for a current automated system. The reason for this is fairly obvious—one should have an idea of the purposes of a task in order to carry it out effectively. It is a minimum requirement that the supervision of the project be carried out by a trained librarian who is familiar with the application of computers to bibliographic processing. It is a grave error to plan such a project or to carry it out without at least this measure of professional knowledge and control. If the other staff engaged in the conversion project are not familiar with library automation and cataloging techniques, then a training system must be evolved. This can be a costly activity but one which will recoup the costs of a good training scheme over and over again during the conversion. This type of activity (a major one-time project) is one where on-the-job training is not at all suitable, and may have dire results. Certain aspects of the BNB conversion have proved this. The training system should embrace not only the techniques to be used in this particular project, but also an overview of the bibliographic standards to be used (or which the project is trying to achieve), and the use to which the converted records are to be put. The editor must be aware of the consequences to the future cataloging system of a particular editing decision. It is particularly important because the editing process, although it can be rendered mechanical to a very great extent, will always have a residue of decisions to be made. To take one very simple example, there is the question of uniform titles (or filing titles) found in some entries. One simply cannot specify the addition of uniform titles or the transference (or nontransference) of uniform titles without understanding the context of the subsequent use of the records.

This has been a brief and necessarily sketchy overview of a large and complex subject, and I can hope to have done no more than to indicate the main strategies and the relative economic consequences to those wishing to convert their back files into machine-readable form.

I would like to thank my colleagues in the British Library, Andrew Phillips and Bruce Royan, for their help during the preparation of this paper.

REFERENCES

1. Jolliffe, John W. "Retrospective Conversion of the British Museum Library Catalogue: Techniques, Strategies and Costs." *In* Department of Education and Science. *The Scope for Automatic Data Processing in the British Library*. London, H.M.S.O., 1972. (Available from National Lending Library for Science and Technology, London, England.)

2. Plaister, Jean. "The LASER/MARC Project," *Catalogue & Index* 34:3-4, Summer/Autumn 1974.

3. RECON Working Task Force. *National Aspects of Creating and Using MARC/RECON Records*. John C. Rather and Henriette D. Avram, eds. Washington, D.C., Library of Congress, 1973.

4. RECON Pilot Project. *RECON Pilot Project; Final Report*. Henriette D. Avram, project dir. Washington, D.C., Library of Congress, 1972.

5. Duchesne, R.M. "Unit Costs of Conversion of Bibliographic Records to Machine-readable Form," Appendix 5 to Annex A: "Cost Estimates for Implementing Recommendations." *In* Department of Education and Science, *op. cit.*, pp. 145-58.

6. RECON Pilot Project, *op. cit.*

7. Jolliffe, John W., dir. *Computers & Early Books: Report of LOC Project*. London, Mansell, 1974.

8. Duchesne, *op. cit.*

VELMA VENEZIANO
Systems Analyst
Northwestern University Library
and
JAMES S. AAGAARD
Associate Professor of Computer Sciences and Electrical Engineering
Northwestern University
Evanston, Illinois

Cost Advantages of Total System Development

The question we will consider in this paper is whether, at the end of a decade of effort to harness computers to the needs of libraries, it is economically feasible and operationally practical for an individual library to design and operate its own in-house automated system. At Northwestern University Library, the answer is both yes and no, but more yes than no.

In his 1975 article, "Library Automation: The Second Decade," Richard DeGennaro says "no." To quote him:

> Many of the premises upon which research libraries based their decisions to build in-house library systems staffs to automate their internal operations in the late 1960's are no longer valid. Important advances in automation have been made, including the widespread acceptance and use of the MARC format and distribution service, the general success of the cooperative network concept, and the availability of package systems. The day of the one-man or small group library systems development effort is past. The jobs to be done and the equipment required have become complex and expensive, and it requires a team of highly qualified computer specialists to design and

> implement a viable system. With the increasing sophistication and success of computerized systems for libraries, the need for systems groups in individual libraries is diminishing.
> The era of localized library automations has effectively come to an end. Experience has shown that it is not economically feasible for any but the very largest libraries to afford the heavy costs of developing, maintaining, and operating complex localized computer-based systems. Many libraries are quietly abandoning this approach in favor of joining networks such as OCLC or its affiliates or purchasing turnkey mini-computer systems from commercial vendors for specific applications.[1]

DeGennaro correctly identifies a trend, but for the wrong reasons. In our judgment, library automation efforts have failed or been minimally effective because libraries have not approached automation realistically.

In the past it was often assumed that a librarian, by simply taking a few courses in data processing, could direct the library's automation effort. Even worse, it was often believed that people from the local computer facility, with no knowledge of libraries, could tackle the problem effectively. There were unrealistic expectations about the time required to do the job, with many administrators believing that a year or two would be sufficient for systems to be developed and to begin paying off in cost savings and improvements in efficiency.

Some libraries underestimated the complexity of the problem; others overestimated it. Using huge staffs paid with grant money, these libraries found that too much staff time was spent attempting to communicate with one another and in writing reports. Under such conditions, the amount of progress tended to be inversely proportional to the number of people involved and the amount of money being spent.

Fortunately, Northwestern has avoided many of these pitfalls. We began our development more than eight years ago with a full-time staff equivalent to one and two-thirds people, which has now grown to two and two-thirds people. With dogged determination and little money or fanfare, we have been making progress, although it sometimes seems to be very slow.

We believe that the Northwestern University Library is more highly automated than any of the large research libraries. Our system was developed with no outside grant money, and the development cost was a fraction of what has gone into the development of some of the other more highly publicized systems. Development costs for the first five-year period were about $300,000, including data conversion costs. For this expenditure we have operational on-line ordering, cataloging, serial check-in, and circulation systems, as well as a batch SDI (selective dissemination of information) system.

Our operational costs are moderate and well within the resources of any large library. Not including terminals, most of which we own, our computer costs are less than $120,000 a year. Considering that we have a book budget of about $1 million, this is not excessive.

We catalog about 40,000 books a year, producing about 500,000 catalog cards and 20,000 purchase orders. We prepare more than 100,000 worksheets and about 12,000 claims in a year. We circulate about 400,000 books, producing fine notices, book-needed and book-available notices, and overdue notices. We print pocket labels and produce punched circulation cards automatically. We check in about 90,000 periodicals yearly, in addition to monographic series.

We do not yet have a true on-line catalog; this is the module which is presently being developed. We do, however, have our entire serial collection—approximately 40,000 titles—on-line, and we have bibliographic data in machine-readable form for about 200,000 monographs.

Our success is due to a combination of factors. In part, we were lucky in having just the right set of conditions at the right time. There are literally hundreds of factors which can influence a project like this; we will try to outline a few of the most important ones.

Economy of Scope

One of the prime rules for an effective and economical in-house automation system is that it be comprehensive. It is essential to realize that there is no single operation performed by the library which, by itself, can be automated economically. Ordering systems, cataloging systems, circulation systems, or serial systems, if designed and operated in isolation from one another, tend to be costly and have minimal impact on overall library efficiency. This realization is behind the mass movement to the Ohio College Library Center (OCLC), which produces catalog cards in phenomenal quantities, thus achieving the objective of "economy of scale."

Because an in-house system cannot take advantage of the "economy of scale" concept, it must be designed to permit "economy of scope." By spreading the costs over a broad base of applications, the cost of any one application can be minimized. From the very first, Northwestern's system was conceived as a "total integrated system," with the objective of eliminating all manual files, including the card catalog. However, it is a very complex task to design and implement a total system. No matter how much money is available and how many people are assigned to the task, there is an irreducible amount of time required to design and implement a system. Unfortunately, library and university administrations, like their counterparts in business and industry, take a dim view of projects which drag on for years without visible results. Next year's appropriations are often dependent on the demonstrated results of the current year. For this reason it is essential that the total system be designed so that it can be implemented in modules.

In addition to using the modular approach, and because of the necessity to establish credibility as a basis for continued funding, it is often necessary to design a first-generation system which does not have all of the "bells and whistles" which we have come to expect of computers. This is a perfectly valid approach, provided one is aware that sooner or later such a "stripped down" system will have to be enhanced. Substantial investments in time and money may be required to make such enhancements.

The cost-effective in-house library system, in addition to being "total" and "modular," must take advantage of every possible money-saving device. The concept of "multiple-use" data is essential to an economical system. For this reason, the separation of systems—circulation from cataloging, for example—is to be avoided. Thus, in an ideal system, a file of call numbers can be used both as circulation control and as a shelflisting tool. This same file becomes a means by which an ongoing inventory of the collection can be maintained, reducing the amount of lost time and annoyance created by lost or misshelved books. The file is valuable for special studies; for instance, we have used our inventory file at Northwestern to help us to evaluate our book loss problem and to project space requirements.

An effective and economical system must also avoid redundant data entry. With an integrated order/catalog system, author, title, and imprint information entered for purposes of ordering can be modified or used "as is" for the cataloging function. However, the avoidance of redundant data entry does not necessarily mean that data redundancy in files is undesirable. We have had to be constantly on guard against designing a system which is wasteful of computer processing time. Our philosophy has been that with computer storage costs declining so much faster than processing costs, reduction of the latter has the greater priority. For example, we have not yet been convinced that complete inversion of bibliographic records is practical. Although we strive to take advantage of data compression techniques wherever possible, we think that some data redundancy is a small price to pay for processing efficiency.

The Northwestern system is not yet a total system, although it more nearly approaches that goal than any we know about in other large research libraries. In its present configuration we cannot claim to have achieved any cost savings; the best we can say is that it costs no more than it would cost to do the job manually. However, it does the job better and faster. We have no way of determining the value of this.

The important thing to stress is that we have established the foundation for moving on to the next module—the on-line catalog. This is the area in which we anticipate the greatest payoff. It is our conclusion that the cost of library operations can be affected substantially by automation only when it enables us to cut off our slavery to the card catalog. As long as technical and public service personnel are tied to this monster, and as long as catalog copy, whether from MARC or not, must be integrated and reconciled with it, then there will be little increase in efficiency.

This brings up something which has become a sore point with the catalogers at our library. They have heard stories of libraries which claim to have greatly increased their cataloging productivity as a result of using the OCLC system. Because we ourselves use MARC copy, acquired automatically from the MARC tapes, we wonder how they have been able to do it. Although we have virtually eliminated the typing and reproduction of catalog cards, thus cutting our clerical costs, we have not been able to cut the cost of the cataloging operation itself. Frankly, we are skeptical of claims of large cost savings. We suspect that the transition to OCLC has given administrators an opportunity to make changes—in organization, in the level of personnel assigned to cataloging, and in work-flow and procedures—which by themselves would have increased productivity. Such improvements did not accompany the changeover to automation at Northwestern because we had already streamlined our cataloging operation.

Our catalogers also wonder if some of these reported cost savings are not being achieved at the cost of an impaired catalog in which the user and public service personnel will pay the price of lost access to materials. Even though we have had to compromise the quality of our cataloging to some degree, we still take reasonable precautions to avoid conflicts with earlier cataloging.

The Objective

We have said that we expect a "total system" to improve greatly our operating efficiency, and if it does not allow us to cut costs, we expect that at least the per-unit cost of processing a book will level off. We also expect that the user will benefit greatly from the system. However, we have not yet defined exactly what this total system will be. We expect it to be an on-line system with a file of bibliographic records for all items either held by the library, on order, or in process. Linked to these bibliographic records are files of local processing and control information—order records, holdings records, circulation records, invoice records, fund records, and patron records. Patrons as well as librarians use the system directly, searching the files by means of any of several access points. The card catalog as a means of access to materials acquired since 1971 is gone; also gone are manual files of orders, bindery records, serial check-in records, and so forth. In their places are terminals, in public areas as well as in the processing areas.

After searching to see if a potential purchase is already held, the decision to order is made. Bibliographic and order records are created at this time, and purchase orders are produced by the system. A commitment is automatically entered against the appropriate fund. When an item is received, whether it is a monograph, a multivolume set, or a single issue of a journal, its receipt is recorded in the order record. A record for each vendor invoice is created and updated automatically as the items on it are checked in. When the sum of the line items balances the total, the invoice is approved for payment and the check is written automatically. Claims for overdue items (books as well as journal issues) are also generated automatically. Using a terminal, catalogers review and update the bibliographic record at the appropriate time and request book materials (labels and punched circulation cards).

Patrons use terminals to search for wanted items; having found them, they can interrogate the circulation file to see if the items are available. Using self-service terminals, patrons charge out their own books. The circulation system takes care of the production of overdue notices, call-in notices, and notices of books available. Although fines are assessed in cases of gross delinquency, for the most part the system is self-regulating, blocking a user from taking out books after he has accumulated a certain number of "demerits."

When we make the transition to a true on-line catalog, enabling searchers and catalogers to search and modify records from a terminal, we estimate that we can achieve about a 30 percent increase in productivity on the part of our technical services staff, both professional and clerical. The savings should be more than enough to offset the additional costs of terminals and computer time.

It is important to point out, however, that there are two aspects of library operations which are not good candidates for an in-house system. The first is the maintenance of a large data base such as the MARC file in an on-line mode. This is completely impractical for a single institution; it must be done on a regional or national basis. At present we maintain and search the MARC file off-line. With the file at its present size (about 600,000 records), we can do this more cheaply than we could if we participated in OCLC. This will become difficult by the time the number of records reaches one million, however, and we sincerely hope that there will be a method of acquiring catalog copy for direct transfer into our files at a reasonable cost.

The other area which makes sense only at the regional or national level is the maintenance of a union file of holdings, one which can be searched in order to locate items for interlibrary loan. However, because the volume of materials which we borrow is relatively low, this has not been an area of major concern. With the steady increase in the cost of purchasing materials, this might become of more interest to us in the future.

Hardware

We will now examine some of the details of the system design, both hardware and software, which have enabled us, with a modest investment, to accomplish what we have.

At the time we started our development effort, we were not aware that the comprehensive system we envisioned could not be implemented on the small IBM/360 Model 30 computer that the university was using for administrative purposes, so we proceeded to do it. (Actually we had little choice.) For data storage we used part of a "data cell" which the university had obtained primarily for storage of alumni records, and we located an inexpensive source of special type balls for our terminals. As we were able to build the administration's confidence in our abilities, we managed to get the computer storage upgraded to 96K and encouraged the replacement of the data cell with disc storage. During the entire project we have been required to justify each increment in computer capability.

Fortunately, we have been aided by advances in computer technology. The Model 30 was replaced by an IBM/370 Model 135, at essentially the same cost but with a substantially increased CPU speed. This helped us to accommodate the steady increase in work load. Further increases in storage were needed to accommodate the teleprocessing monitor program (CICS) which we later elected to use. At the present time, this computer has 192K of storage, and we estimate that one more small increase will be enough for our growth in the next two years.

We emphasize that this is not a dedicated library computer; it is used for all university administrative data processing, and this is during the first shift hours when library usage is heaviest. For this reason our response time sometimes slips below what we would like it to be, but we know that we are not alone with this problem. We conducted a study a few years ago to compare our charges with the costs of a dedicated computer. The university charges our account approximately $120,000 per year for data processing services. This amount includes batch processing for catalog cards and purchase orders, batch processing for SDI services, batch processing for program development, and teleprocessing charges (see Table 1). By doing all library batch processing on the second shift, when the teleprocessing load is much lighter, we felt that an IBM/370 Model 115 with the same amount of storage could handle the load of the library system alone, and we found that the cost of such a system was almost identical to what we were being charged by the university. The university was understandably not willing to let us make this change, bcause there was no way the cost of the administrative computer could be reduced by $120,000 if the library pulled out. However, we think this does illustrate that it is possible for a library to have a system like ours, even if a computer which can be shared is not available.

In fact, library applications tend to require a relatively large amount of storage, both in the computer and externally, and relatively low computation speeds. For this reason it is quite possible that a library which shares a large, high-speed computer encumbered by a complicated operating system may be paying for computing power which it does not really need. We cannot offer any data to support this thought, because the opportunity has never been available to us, but we would caution you, especially in this day of what one manufacturer calls the "megaminicomputer," not to overlook what can be done with a relatively small computer.

We have tried very hard to avoid efforts to develop special hardware. This has caused inconveniences in several areas, particularly in the entering and display of special characters in bibliographic records, and in providing a reliable output device for our self-service circulation terminals. Development of hardware of this type can be very expensive and time-consuming, for it requires expertise in all areas of computer science, from electronic circuits to data communications and operating systems. The problems with the circulation terminal finally became sufficiently annoying that we entered into an agreement with a group within the university to develop a new terminal. This development has been in process for more than a year, and we have yet to see an operational prototype. We have not given up hope, but this experience has reinforced our determination that hardware development is to be done only as an absolute last resort.

Another recommendation is to deal with as few vendors as possible. The computer trade press likes to headline the dollars which can be saved by "shopping around" for computer hardware, but for a small installation these dollars may not be worth the annoyance. A large computing center, with dozens of tape and disc drives, may be able to save more than enough to pay the salary of the hardware specialist who can draw up specifications, help with selection, and then pinpoint which vendor's equipment is the cause of a particular system failure. Again, we have not been able to follow our own advice completely; our hardware comes from three different vendors (if the telephone company is included). Our experience, however, reinforces our recommendation that this is a situation to be avoided if possible; the savings of $5,000 or $10,000 a year is not sufficient reason to add another vendor.

It must also be decided whether to buy or lease the equipment. There is no question that purchase or a long-term lease can save a considerable amount of money if the equipment will be used for a period of five or more years. Hindsight indicates that we, and our university, have not always made the best decision in this respect. Although the CPU represents the largest single cost in the total hardware budget, a short-term lease—or a long-term lease with appropriate contractual provisions—will facilitate the gradual expansion of the system as the various modules are implemented. The other

Function	*Processing Charge*		*Terminal Cost*
	Batch	*Teleprocessing*	
Circulation and Public Services	$16,000	$17,700	$21,500
Technical Services	27,000	41,500	18,000
SDI	13,500		
Development	1,500		4,000
TOTALS	$58,000	$59,200	$43,500

Table 1. Computer costs for Northwestern University Library, 1974-75

alternative is to pay for more initial capability than is needed and hope that someone else doesn't make use of it before the library needs it.

On the other hand, the peripheral devices seem to be more suitable for a long-term commitment. Tape and disc drives and terminals can be used with different computer models, and more units can be added without affecting the status of those already in operation. In our case our biggest mistake was in not purchasing our circulation terminals, which we have had for over six years; the primary reason for leasing was that we kept hoping that something more suitable would appear.

There is one other criterion which can be applied: as a general rule it is safer to make a long-term commitment to equipment which has just been introduced than to devices which have been in the field for several years. Special consideration is necessary if the new equipment comes from a new vendor—will the vendor still be in business in five years to provide parts and service?

Software

It is, of course, the software which can make or break a system, and it is here that the system designer is faced with a bewildering array of choices. Should it be written in the library, in the computing center, or contracted with an outside vendor? Should you try to incorporate existing data management or communication management packages into the system? Should the programs be written in assembly language, COBOL, or PL/I?

To answer the last question first, the combination of the complexities of bibliographic data and an on-line environment almost dictates programming in assembly language. There is no doubt that this requires a more highly skilled staff and raises the initial cost of the programs, but this money is recovered over and over again in the daily use of these programs. A well-designed assembly language program will occupy much less storage itself, require less execution time, and often permit compression of data, as compared with a program written in some other language.

The decision whether to purchase generalized system components, such as data base management systems, or telecommunications monitors is less clear. Available packages must be examined to determine how closely they fit the library's requirements, whether they will operate on available hardware, and their cost. For example, we found that the capability to process variable length fields usually was lacking in the data base management systems we investigated. On the other hand, capabilities which are included in the package but which are not required by the library can substantially increase the hardware needed to operate them.

A few years ago we elected to modify our system to operate under the IBM telecommunications monitor system called CICS. We are still uncertain whether this was a wise decision. The package is widely used, its price is reasonable, and it appears efficient. It is also difficult to learn and uses much of the computer storage. We have not acquired any data base management system; most of them are poorly suited to bibliographic data and we feel that their price far outweighs any benefits. We are, however, using IBM's new VSAM (virtual storage access method) for file management. This is undoubtedly an improvement over the old indexed sequential system, but still appears to be overly general, much less efficient than it could be, and grossly wasteful of storage. Fortunately, file management is a well-defined part of the whole system, so that if something better comes along, or if we have the time to develop something ourselves, it should be possible to incorporate it without a major impact on the overall system.

The idea of acquiring a complete library system seems attractive, but there are few, if any, to be found. A system like ours, which is economical to operate because it is designed to do exactly what we want it to do and no more, would undoubtedly require extensive modification by another library. A very generalized system, designed to provide for the needs of a variety of libraries, would be costly to buy (because it would be costly to design) and costly to operate. A good compromise would be a modular system for which the purchaser could select certain modules and easily modify others. A truly modular system is also expensive to design, but as we have mentioned earlier, the modular approach is desirable for other reasons. We have tried to follow this approach as much as possible, and we suspect that if another library were to acquire our programs, it could use the bibliographic modules almost unchanged; the holdings modules might require minor changes, and the ordering and accounting modules would need major changes. This situation, of course, reflects the influence of the MARC project on the library world.

The idea of contracting with some other organization to design and develop the system might be attractive—if the money were available and there were no other way to obtain the staff with the necessary qualifications. We have never seriously considered this alternative. It tends to remove the designers from the close contact with the eventual users which we feel is important. It requires that every last detail of the system specifications be put in writing to avoid misunderstandings, and this in turn inhibits the implementers from making minor modifications to the specifications, modifications which may result in a substantial saving in development or operational cost.

Staff and Organization

One of the reasons that the Northwestern automation effort has been relatively successful is that we have had good access to a small group of people who would have to use the system—we could get agreement from them about what the system should include and what it should not. It is much easier to please 5 users than it is to please 500, or even 50.

For the staff of such a project, it is necessary to find either librarians with an interest in computers and a willingness to learn more, or computer experts with an interest in libraries or text processing and a willingness to learn more. It does not work, and we can say this from experience, to assign a program to print catalog cards to a person who has spent his whole career writing COBOL programs to do payroll tasks. The frustrations encountered in trying to locate the right people are only exceeded by the frustrations in trying to do the project without them.

Our design and development staff has been small and cohesive, and able to make and implement decisions quickly. It has had full administrative support. It is organized in a staff, rather than line, capacity, with all administrative, managerial, and operational tasks assigned to other departments in the library. We have made special efforts to maintain good relations with other members of the library staff and to secure their participation in the design. They have been encouraged to take full responsibility for the operation of modules of the system at the earliest possible time, and have done so.

Cost Advantages of the Total System

So far, we have really not provided much justification for the possible cost advantages of a single-institution in-house system as compared with participation in a network. The comparison with network operation is difficult to make. There is only one network for which cost data are available, and that is OCLC. The real problem, however, is that the services are not comparable, so we must either attempt to isolate the part of our costs related only to the production of catalog cards, or else estimate what OCLC might charge for producing purchase orders, serial check-in, and so forth. Using the first basis, we find that our costs are approximately equal to those of OCLC. We feel that the balance will shift in our favor when additional services are included.

Why should this be true? Primarily because there is much less redundancy in the data associated with the additional services than there is in bibliographic information. Libraries are willing to accept bibliographic records created elsewhere, but they are not likely to be able to use order or circulation records of another institution. By centralizing such records, there is little saving in storage costs and a considerable increase in communication costs. The possible savings in using a large computer rather than several smaller ones are often lost in higher overhead costs, both in the computer software and in personnel to operate it. When a library decides to make an on-line catalog available to its patrons, the communication costs will increase several times, and it may then prove more economical to maintain even bibliographic files locally.

As we said earlier, we feel that there is definitely a place for large networks in providing access to bibliographic information and for interlibrary loan purposes. However, we firmly believe that other types of information should be maintained on an individual basis by large libraries, or perhaps by small groups of small libraries.

REFERENCE

1. De Gennaro, Richard. "Library Automation: The Second Decade," *Journal of Library Automation* 8:3-4, March 1975.

S. MICHAEL MALINCONICO
Assistant Chief
Systems Analysis and Data Processing Office
The New York Public Library

The Economics of Computer Output Media

Information not transferred to some sentient recipient is of no particular value, at least of no direct concern to us in this clinic. A library is in simplest terms merely a warehouse for information, albeit information in a very particular form: in recorded form. Our concern at this clinic is with methods of delivering information to a user or, more accurately, information about the information contained in the warehouse. Information can only be transmitted by effecting a modulation in some medium. These modulations can be divided into two classes: those which are primarily temporal, and those which are primarily spatial. As with any such simple model, the distinctions are never so clear in practice. Nonetheless, we can speak of temporally modulated messages as short-duration messages (e.g., sound waves carrying language, or light waves carrying images), while printed information might be thought of as spatial modulations used to encode characters on some medium. It should be obvious that long-duration messages must be transduced into short-duration messages before they can be received by a human. The advantages of long-duration messages are obvious: the activity necessary to synthesize new information from primitive elements must be performed only once; the products of this synthesis can be delivered to many users separated in space and time from each other and from the author; and furthermore, users can choose to accept the information when they are ready to do so. While long-duration messages permit efficient and economical distribution of information, this advantage is decreasing as a result of advances in computers.

In many library applications, a computer serves merely to convert one particular kind of long-duration information into a form more easily converted into short-duration messages for human consumption. The actual process, of course, might involve several intermediate transformations into long- and short-duration messages. Computer processing speeds have tended to blur these distinctions. Consider, for instance, the CRT display. Such a display does indeed make use of spatial modulation in producing its messages; however, because of the medium upon which the spatial modulation is effected, it must be refreshed every thirty milliseconds, thus introducing elements of temporality. Because of the virtually infinite reusability of the medium, messages can moreover be produced for time periods much shorter than those normally associated with a spatially modulated form. This naturally gives rise to the possibility of interactive query. Because of the remarkable speed with which long-duration information can be encoded (data entry) and displayed (data access), and the virtually infinitesimal time delay between encoding and access, another dimension to the information transfer process is added—currency of information.

There is no question about the importance or sophistication of on-line CRT systems. The principal drawback is simply their cost. In judging their value one must carefully analyze the use to which they are put; for example, the value of the searcher's time must be quantified, as must the value of the immediacy of the data. This analysis is often extremely complex. One must necessarily include in these considerations the expected time a potential user must wait for access to the relatively expensive resources (terminals, transmission lines, CPU, etc.) required to make use of such facilities. Such analyses, in many cases, need no longer be reduced to first principles. Observation of the results of experiments carried out in similar situations can greatly simplify this process.

In most cases in which interactive systems are in wide use, the results are generally favorable. The value of enhanced service and the diminution of other easily quantified costs justify the cost of these systems. This, of course, is very similar to demonstrations of the validity of hypotheses in theories of evolution—if they weren't valid, the species under discussion wouldn't be there: *ergo, quod erat demonstrandum.*

Let us quickly review some of the elements which go into determining the cost of an on-line system. For the duration of activity a user must have access to: the terminal display station (costs about $4,000 to purchase, plus $50/month for maintenance), telephone line (about $1/month/mile), computer with peripheral devices to support the telecommunications system (about $25,000/month depending on configuration), and direct access auxiliary storage (about $10,000/month for two million records).

With the exception of the display stations, each of these facilities can generally serve several users with the appearance of simultaneity. Shared facilities might accommodate from 50 users on a telephone line to 500 users sharing a computer system. The illusion of simultaneity is generally quite successful until response time becomes appreciable. Nonetheless, the ability of modern computer systems to multiplex large numbers of users has tended to make them cost-justifiable despite the costs involved sounding astronomic. Although costs are relatively high today, they are showing a marked tendency to decrease. For example, the sort of terminal necessary for library cataloging cost about $7,000 in 1972; an improved model now costs about $4,000. Additionally, intense competition among data communication services is rapidly lowering the cost of data transmission.

Nonetheless, I would like to devote the remainder of this discussion to a consideration of the more traditional, relatively static, spatially modulated forms of information display as provided by print technology. The various forms of print technology have been, and still are, characterized by a significantly lower basic price for carrying long-duration messages. They suffer from an inability to provide rapid and interactive access to, and currency or immediacy of, data. The rapidly decreasing costs for various types of "printed" products are providing the means for ameliorating these drawbacks to some extent. Declining costs, of course, cannot themselves provide such direct assistance for the problem of rapid access. However, indexing techniques are helping in some media to solve them; we shall return to this point later. Currency of printed information can, of course, be improved by more frequently producing the publication containing it.

As we know, only a small fraction of a library collection is consulted by users in any given brief span of time. The same is true of a printed catalog or, for that matter, of any list. The problem in both cases is that no one can predict which items will be sought by a user at some time in the future. Thus, the printed list, like a research library collection, attempts within limits to *pre-respond* to all requests which might be lodged against it. This is the generic problem plaguing all extremely long-duration information; because it is produced, or acquired, only once, it must be kept available in case it is needed.

If we are to derive the maximum advantage from long-duration information, it must satisfy a large number of users. Because of the unpredictable nature of a potential user's information requirements, information encoded in long-duration form must attempt to pre-answer as many queries as possible. As a natural corollary, the larger the number of questions one attempts to pre-answer, the larger the number of answers which satisfy *no query* lodged against them; thus, the greater the waste margin. The necessity for a large waste margin is an inescapable characteristic of any information system that relies on recorded information; this is observed in all studies of collection usage, and has been highlighted again by statistics on the use of MARC records. Few institutions find any need for even 30 percent of the records distributed by the Library of Congress (LC); in fact, the Ohio College Library Center's (OCLC) experience, in which a large number of libraries attempt to utilize MARC, has shown that about one-half of all LC MARC records remain unused. The expense of providing a waste margin imposes a constraint on the level of service a system can provide. In the case of library collections, we try to limit the waste margin by exercising a policy of collection development. In a card catalog we limit the number of added entries because of the expense of producing and filing additional cards. In a book-form catalog produced by automated methods, the constraints are considerably less severe, but nonetheless present.

Because several media are suitable for recording cataloging information, we can seek one which minimizes the constraints it imposes. Let me apologize for a certain looseness in the use of the term *media*. A computer-based system, regardless of the medium chosen for display of information, is itself a medium. The display medium may in some cases impose constraints on the total system, with the effect of preventing data processing technology from being used to its full potential. For example, a computer can easily completely reorganize a catalog, but if the display medium consists of printed 3 X 5-inch cards we cannot easily make use of this facility, because the changes are not automatically reflected in the manual catalog. An on-line system, on the other hand, makes the results of additions to (or reorganization of) the catalog directly available to users.

Book-form catalogs have a similar capability for making the results of a catalog's reorganization easily available to users. The schedule chosen for publication, however, can limit the effectiveness of rapid reorganization to the user. For instance, if a book-form catalog is published as a complete cumulation each time, then all of the changes are available to the user at the time of publication. The drawback is that the user must wait for the next publication period. On the other hand, a catalog published as a cumulation plus supplements necessarily implies both several look-ups and the presence of both the old form in a cumulation and the changed form in a supplement—until a new cumulation is issued. A catalog published as cumulation plus supplements, being cheaper than one published as complete cumulations, can be published more frequently. In this way new information can be delivered to the user with greater frequency, improving the timeliness of the catalog.

Supplements to a printed catalog can be in various forms: they can be cumulative, embodying all actions taken since the last issuance of a cumulation, or they can be chronological, representing only those actions taken since the last supplement. The advantages and disadvantages of each are obvious. Cumulative supplements limit the number of alphabets which must be consulted, but are more costly than chronological supplements. Cumulative supplements tend to grow linearly; that is, the second will be twice as large as the first, the third three times as large, etc. Thus, if we assume an input rate R, the total cost for n supplements will be proportional to $n(n+1)R$. That is, the total cost depends on the square of the number of supplements. Here the constant of proportionality depends on the cost of printing an item. Therefore, the costs associated with a particular printed medium can be instrumental in influencing a decision regarding the suitability of a publication scheme.

In this simple exercise we have noted the effect that the choice of output medium can have on the fulfillment of service goals. We have considered only the number of independent look-ups required of a user and the timeliness of the information. Another factor that determines the cost of printing is the number of access points provided. More access points generally improve the service, although too many access points can be self-defeating because the size and complexity of the listing may discourage users.

Nonetheless, our concern is only with the constraints caused by the medium and how they may be relaxed. Thus, if we have an inexpensive form in which to produce a list, we can approach the *functional* limit of added access points. Here again we should note the importance of the underlying medium (computer storage) in making such a choice. If the data were not in machine-readable and hence machine-manipulable form, the cost of creating the alternate access points would greatly overshadow the cost of the display medium. Often, automated systems can provide alternate access points with little effort, because the computer can be programmed to analyze the data and provide them automatically. Examples of simple machine-generated alternate access are seen in KWIC and KWOC indexes. KWIC indexes tend to produce a great many entries, too many to print economically in most applications. They are consequently not provided, not because of computer limitations in producing them or their value to users, but simply because of the cost of the resulting display. An inexpensive medium could easily reverse these considerations. Such a list could help, for example, to ameliorate the problems caused by arcane forms of entry. The University of California at Berkeley, for instance, produces KWIC indexes to the California university union list of serials. They can afford to do so because the list is produced by computer, and on microfiche.

Thus, we should see by now that the economics of output media can generally influence more than an institution's budget. Economic considerations usually impose explicit or implicit constraints on the service one can provide. In the case of printed media, at least, we do have many interesting options from which to choose, some of which can dramatically relax the economic constraints. We can, of course, adopt one of them simply to lower costs. The real promise, however, lies in lowering costs while simultaneously increasing service. For the remainder of this discussion we shall concentrate only on the cost of producing a specified output product. Potential service enhancements will be left to your own creativity and imagination—indeed, some very fertile suggestions have already been put forward by the other speakers.

Let us begin by reviewing some of the traditional options available for printed output. The simplest and most fundamental, when dealing with a computer-based system, is high-speed line printer output. Two basic components determine its cost: (1) the cost of the computer time needed to print the list, and (2) the cost of the forms on which it is printed. The cost of extracting a list from a data base is generally independent of output medium, hence we can ignore it in further considerations. First, some basic figures should be noted. Single-ply paper costs about $9.10/M sheets. All upper-case printing can be done at about 1100 lines/minute; upper-lower-case printing cuts this rate to about 550 lines/minute; and diacritics can further reduce printing speed to approximately 300 lines/minute. The reduction of speed in the latter case is the result of two factors: (1) the American Library Association (ALA) print train, adopted as a library standard, contains the complete range of characters found necessary for the representation of bibliographic data (169 characters). Because of the presence of so many unique graphics, it does not permit common characters to be repeated as often as on simpler trains. Printing time is consequently increased; (2) the print train utilizes floating diacritics, i.e. diacritics (e.g., umlaut, *accent grave*) appear as single independent graphics. In order to produce *ä, ö,* or *ü,* one first prints the alphabetic character and then overprints the diacritic. The figure of 300 lines/minute represents only what we have found at the New York Public Library (NYPL) for our printed lists of bibliographic data, with our mixture of languages; slightly more than one-half of our material is not in English.

High-speed printer output is certainly the most economical way of producing a single copy of a listing, but that's the catch—a single copy. As mentioned above, long-duration information is generally economical to produce only when it can serve many users. Thus, the real problem is to find an economical method to produce printed information in multiple copies. The crudest method of creating several copies of a printed report is to print it several times by rerunning the program. This is patently ludicrous, especially if the list is large and a significant number of copies are required. There are less costly options, such as creating a print-image tape and reprinting the list from it. The most popular method of producing limited numbers of copies of lists is to use special line-printer forms which have carbon paper or "no-carbon" paper to transfer the image imprinted on the first copy to other copies. Four-ply paper costs approximately $36.50/M sheets, or slightly more than four times the cost of single-ply paper. Larger numbers of copies can be produced in this way. Eight-ply paper can be ordered as a special item from most paper vendors, although the legibility limit seems to be reached at the fourth carbon copy, with the fourth copy only marginally usable. When this technique is economically justified, it is common to combine the use of multi-ply paper with reprinting the list. Aside from considerations of legibility, there are other problems and hidden costs associated with this technique. First, the multi-part listing must be decollated. This necessitates a decollating machine and personnel to oversee the operation of this machine. Second, a box of four-ply paper generally contains 750 individual pages, compared to 3700 pages in a box of single-ply paper. This means that computer operators will need to make form changes about five times as often, and the computer partition assigned to the printing task must remain idle while this is being done. Third, special forms must be stored and ordered; if not treated as a cost consideration, this is certainly an ingredient in maintaining amicable relations with your computer center's manager. Finally, because of the need for a special form, the print job may have to wait until that time of the workday when such jobs are run.

The second most popular method relies on making electrostatic copies of a single, clean copy produced by a high-speed printer. This has the advantages of legibility and size reduction which make the listing easier to handle and to house. The major drawback of this technique is the need for a special copying machine. This problem can be solved by using a service bureau for the actual copying process. Xerography, however, has the unfortunate property that no significant advantage is realized for additional copies. Each copy costs about the same, regardless of how many are made. A typical cost for xerographic copying is about 3.8 cents per page. If we assume a listing which requires the full ALA character set (thus having a printing speed of about 300 lines/minute), and that foreground printing time on a computer is valued at $45.00/hour, then for twenty-six or more copies xerography is more economical than using four-ply paper and reprinting the list until the requisite number of copies are made.

For large numbers of paper copies a printing press is hard to surpass for economy, quality, and acceptability of the product. Printing plates can be made photographically from line-printer output. Because the process is photographic, all of the flexibilities of copy reduction which a lens can afford are available. Costs can vary signficantly, depending on the "make ready" steps involved and the grade of paper chosen for the final printed product. Typical costs for such a process, in which there is no manual intervention performed on the copy before printing, are 2 cents/page for the first 100 copies, and .3 cents/page for additional 100s. This compares very favorably with xerographic copies, if only fifty copies are required.

When many copies of a large listing are required and turnaround time is not too critical, another technique is available: phototypesetting with offset printing. In order to use this technique, a photocomposed image of the page must first be created. This is then used in the creation of a printing plate. Camera-ready copy adds about $1.00 to the cost of each page, provided that your own software is capable of creating a driver tape for the photocomposition device (if not, this cost can easily be two times higher). This seems like a significant overhead; however, dramatic reductions can be effected in the number of pages. This has a salutary effect on the total cost of printing, as well as creating a more compact publication more conveniently used. We have found that the number of pages in a book-form catalog can be reduced by a factor of nearly two by photocomposing it. The reasons are simple: less important data can be set in a smaller type size, proportional spacing is used for each character (that is, a lower-case letter *i* requires less space than an upper-case *M*), and white space between entries can be made less than a full line. Variability in type face and size can also be used to other advantage. For instance, as we have already pointed out, detailed information, which is of no value to the user scanning a page for an entry likely to satisfy individual requirements, can be set in smaller type. The primary sequencing element (author, title, subject) that the user is attempting to scan very rapidly can be set in boldface type, thereby making a search through a large number of entries on a page more efficient. Finally, important elements (e.g., the call number) can be highlighted—in italics, for example. The principal qualitative advantage of photocomposed output is, of course, its almost unlimited range of character sets. The full ALA character set is generally available as a standard option. In fact, the New York Public Library (NYPL) Research Libraries' catalog, which is photocomposed, is produced each month with Hebrew text in the vernacular script. Hebrew character data did not increase photocomposition price! Figure 1 shows a page of the catalog with Hebrew text.

In addition to greater variety in character sets, photocomposition offers the advantage of high information density. For example, a typical 12-inch diagonal CRT screen can only display 1,920 characters. An 8½X11-inch photocomposed page can hold 8,000 characters. Reducing this to characters per square inch, we have twenty-seven characters/square inch for a CRT, and eighty-five characters/square inch on a photocomposed page, or at least three times the amount of information within the reader's range of vision.

With a fixed overhead for typesetting, we can expect another crossover point. As I have pointed out, at NYPL we achieved a twofold reduction in the number of pages in a catalog by phototypesetting it. Because of reduction, we find that for more than 150 copies, photocomposed output is more economical than offset printing from photoreduced line-printer copy. We can further determine that for more than fifty-five copies, phototypesetting and printing is more economical than xeroxing.

We can summarize the foregoing by noting the number of copies appropriate for each of the techniques thus far discussed (see the Appendix for detailed calculations):

א. ז. הופיין.
Mani, Menasheh, 1889-
ת[ל] א[ביב] אגרת,729 [1969]
69 p. NN 75-4195052 LC 73-953160
[*PWZ (Hoofien) 75-266]

א. קהלת. ב. סבלו של דור.
Broshi, Zelig, 1907- [New York, 1964] 24 p. NN 74-4877056 LC 74-950592
[*PBM p. v. 991]

אבא שלי בחיל האויר.
Dayan, David.
[תל-אביב] עם עובד [1973]
22 p. NN 75-4265861 LC 74-951369
[*PXLB 75-837]

אבולוציה ויהדות.
Korman, Abraham, 1917-
תל-אביב, [הפצה: ספרייתי]730 [1970]
392 p. NN 75-4507194 LC 76-952906
[*PNK 75-4385]

אבותינו ספרו.
Rabi, Mosheh. (comp)
ירושלים, בקאל,730 [1969 or 70]
320 p. NN 75-4175505 LC 74-954562
[*PRW 75-794]

אבי.
Cohen-Shure, Yehudith, 1942-
תל-אביב, ספרית תחביב [1969]
84 p. NN 75-4195026 LC 74-951378
[*PSF 75-792]

אביהו [פלד. לזכרו ולזכר קרב ירושלים.
כנרת, קבוצת כנרת, 1968]
[60] p. illus., facsims., map, ports. 21 cm.
Cover title. NN 75-4391793 LC 70-950247
[*PWZ (Peled, A.) 75-2269]

ספר אבן ספיר.
Sapir, Jacob, 1822-1886.
ירושלים, ספרית מקורותי,730 [1969 or 70]
3 v. in 1. NN 75-4177749 LC 73-200698
[*PWD 75-778]

אבן-שעות.
Hazaz, Haim, 1898-1973.
תל אביב, עם עובד [1973]
236 p. NN 75-4160910 LC 73-950271
[*PSI 75-856]

ספר אבני בית היוצר.
Weiss, Izsák, 1874-1942.
ירושלים, 730 [1970]
11, 86, [7] l. NN 75-4188463 LC 78-953286
[*PWN 75-759]

אבני צדק.
Panet, Menahem Mendel, d. 1884.
ספרי שאלות ותשובות שערי צדק על אר"ח
ויו"ד; אבני צדק על אבה"ע; משפט צדק על
חושי"מ, מאת מנחם מענדל פאנעט. ברוקלין,
ישיבת מעגלי צדק-דעעש,731 [1970 or 71]
4 v. in 1. NN 75-4418727 LC 73-212162
[*PIZ 75-2305]

ספר אבני שיש.
Rotman, Shalom Ya'akov Simḥah.
ירושלים, יו"ל ע"ל בני וחתני המחבר,730
[1970]
208, 22 p. NN 75-4168687 LC 70-952453
[*PHY 75-765]

אבנים בחומה.
Cohen, Raphael Hayyim, 1883-
ירושלים, הוצאת דפוס ר. ח. הכהן,730
[1969 or 70]
11, 184 p. NN 75-4590567 LC 77-952172
[*PWZ (Cohen, R. H.) 75-5536]

אבנר לורד. [עין-דור, קיבוץ עין-דור, 730
i. e. 1969 or 70] 63 p. illus. 21 x 25 cm.
Cover title:
אבנר.
NN 75-4216705 LC 73-950178
[*PWZ (Lord) 75-270]

אבק חוצות.
Chomsky, Dov, 1912-
רמת-גן, מסדה [1972]
121 p. NN 74-4913953 LC 72-950472
[*PSF 74-4928]

אבק רוחות.
Ben-Ner, Asaf.
[תל-אביב] אל"ף [1972]
[30] p. NN 74-4913991 LC 72-950154
[*PSF 74-4923]

אברהם ברקוביץ; דפים לזכרו, שנה למותו.
עינת, 728 [1968]
52 p. illus., ports. 21 cm. NN 75-4168714 LC HE68-3310
[*PWZ (Berkovits) 75-754]

אברהם העברי.
Livne, Zvi, 1891-
תל-אביב, עם עובד [1973]
236 p. NN 75-4456157 LC 73-952650
[*PDY (Abraham) 75-834]

אברהם סוצקעווערס פאעטישער וועג.
Mark, Yudel, 1897-1975.
תל-אביב, פארלאג י. ל. פרץ, 1974.
176 p. NN 75-4561275 LC 74-951096
[*PAY (Sutzkever) 75-4471]

אבשלום.
Feinberg, Absalom, 1889-1917.
חיפה, שקמונה [1971]
382 p. NN 75-4560704 LC 70-954498
[*PBP 75-4498]

אגדות המקום.
Luz, Tsevi.
[תל-אביב] עקד [1972]
171 p. NN 74-4913965 LC 72-951013
[*PSI 74-4927]

אגדת הבקעה וההר ועוד סיפורים [מאת]
אמציה פורת.
Porat, Amazya, 1932-
[תל-אביב, קצין חינוך ראשי, ענף השכלה,
1969]
106 p. NN 75-4195177 LC 70-951594
[*PSI 75-818]

אגודת "פרדס" בת 70: תר"ס 1900-תש"ל,
1970. [עריכה: א. עבר-הדני. תל-אביב,
אגודת פרדס,
730 i. e. 1970] 107 p. illus. 21 x 28 cm.
Added t. p.: Seventieth anniversary of Pardess: 1900-1970. Summary in English. NN 74-4789667 LC 72-950219
[*PYM 74-3782]

אגרות רבי יצחק אייזיק הלוי.
Halevy, Isaak, 1847-1914.
ירושלים, מוסד הרב קוק [1972]
208 p. NN 75-4177751 LC 72-950527
[*PWZ (Halevy, I.) 75-768]

אגרותי אל דורות אחרים.
Silberschlag, Eisig, 1903-
ירושלים, קרית-ספר [1971]
203 p. NN 74-4913977 LC 72-954078
[*PSF 74-4925]

ספר אגרת בקורת ...
Emden, Jacob Israel ben Zebi, 1697-1776.
ירושלים, מכון חתם סופר;
[Brooklyn, High College "Rabbi Akiba Eiger," 730 [1969 or 70] 76 (i. e. 68) p. NN 74-4789617 LC 70-952934
[*PIQ 74-2712]

אדום ולבן וריח תפוחי הזהב [הפואמה
הפדגוגית של] "ילדי טהראן." ערך, כינס
ותירגם בן-ציון תומר. ירושלים, הספריה
הציונית,732 [1971]
20, 15-328 p. illus. 23 cm.
"סיפורם האישי ... על-ידם או מפיהם.
NN 75-4507170 LC 74-954432
[*PXK 75-4387]

אדי אשד.
Zines, Yafa.
[תל-אביב] אל"ף [1971]
47 p. NN 74-4913989 LC 71-953662
[*PSF 74-4924]

אדי-חלום.
Shenhar, 'Alizah.
[תל-אביב] אל"ף [1970]
46 p. NN 74-4876357 LC 70-953469
[*PSF 74-3814]

אדם בערבה.
Kushnir, Simon, 1896-
[תל אביב] עם עובד [1973]
220 p. NN 75-4361497 LC 74-950877
[*PWZ (Almog) 75-1465]

אדם ועולמו, מאת הוראציוס ... ועוד.
[ציורים: ת. פלודי. כתב ועריכה גראפית:
אמציה כ"ץ. ליקוט: א. ב. ביצוע: מריצה
רוסמן. תל-אביב, עקד, 1967]
[23] l. col. illus. 12 cm. Partially vocalized. NN 75-4590606 LC HE68-4498
[*PRY 75-5548]

אדם מתחת רק פעמיים.
Avidar-Ettinger, Tammar.
רמת-גן, מסדה [1971]
205 p. NN 75-4489790 LC 78-954240
[*PSK 75-3397]

אדמומית של סתיו.
Nedava, Joseph. (comp)
[תל-אביב] רשפים [1969]

88 p. NN 75-4660124 LC 74-951690
[*PSN 75-5529]

ספר אהבה וברכה.
Yelin, Shemu'el Ḥayim.
ירושלם, 729
[1968 or 9? 8 (i. e. 10) 150 p. NN 75-4532820 LC 77-952200
[*PLH 75-3424]

אהוד רפמן; נפל בקרבות שכם במלחמת
ששת הימים. [ניר-דוד] קיבוץ השומר הצעיר
ניר-דוד (תל-עמל), 1968.
95 p. illus., facsims., ports. 23 cm.
"מתוך צרור מכתביו":
p. [75]-83. NN 75-4195040 LC 70-950741
[*PWZ (Rafman) 75-268]

אהל אברהם.
Elimelech, of Lezajsk, 1717-1787.
ספר אהל אלימלך [מאת אלימלך מליזענסק.
ספר] אהל אברהם [מאת אברהם אביש,
אב"ד פראנקפורט דמיין. לקוטי חידושי תורה
ושיחות עם סיפורים והנהגות, אספתי
ולקטתי אברהם חיים שמחה בונם
מיכלזאהן. ירושלים? 1967 or 8]
2 v. in 1. NN 75-4166481 LC 71-950084
[*PQZ 75-751]

אהל אברהם. קונטרס אהל אברהם לזכר ...
אברהם הלוי לבקוביץ ליום השנה הראשון
לפטירתו; כולל חידושים וביאורים בסוגיות
הש"ס ומפרשיו מאתו ומאת ידידיו ותלמידיו
... ודברי הספד שנאמרו ביום השלשים
לפטירתו. [נערך ע"י משה דוד אורליק]
בני-ברק, ת"ת "ר' עקיבא,"727 [1967]
62 p. NN 75-4422803 LC HE68-3657
[*PHY 75-2374]

ספר אהל אלימלך.
Elimelech, of Lezajsk, 1717-1787.
[ירושלים? 1967 or 8]
2 v. in 1. NN 75-4166481 LC 71-950084
[*PQZ 75-751]

אהרקע דער ליטוואק.
Chinitz, Joshua.
ניו-יארק
[Alef farlag] 1972 [i.e. 1973] ix, 393 p. NN 74-4914222 LC 74-950000
[*PTR 74-4926]

די אוהאמאס.
Zigelboym, Feivel.
[תל-אביב, פארלאג י. ל. פרץ, 1971]
220 p. NN 74-4914234 LC 72-953866
[*PTR 74-4967]

אוטוביאוגרפיה זמנית.
Dayan, Asaf.
[תל-אביב] עקד [1973]
[28] p. NN 74-4914006 LC 74-950147
[*PSF 74-4921]

אוטוביוגרפיה.
Aranne, Zalman, 1899-1970.
תל-אביב] עם עובד [1971]
203 p. NN 75-4492052 LC 73-954109
[*PWZ (Aranne) 75-4330]

אוטומציה.
Jerusalem. Central School of Administration.
[ירושלים, הוצאת השירות להשכלה
ולהדרכה] 1967.
1 v. (various pagings) NN 75-4168702 LC HE68-3485
[*PVQ 75-743]

אויסגעבענקט.
Baumwoll, Rokhl, 1913-
תל-אביב, פארלאג י. ל. פרץ, 1972.
199 p. NN 74-4914094 LC 72-950085
[*PTN 74-4968]

אויסגעחלומטער ניגון.
Zaretsky, Hinde, 1899-
ניו-יארק, 1973.
128 p. NN 74-4914208 LC 73-212919
[*PTN 74-4969]

אויסדויער.
Binecki, Pesah.
תל-אביב, [תרבות לעם] 1963.
259 p. NN 74-4914133 LC 77-259266
[*PTN 74-4970]

אויף די ראנדן פון תנ"ך.
Olitzky, Leib, 1894-
[תל-אביב] אשל, 1969.
165 p. NN 74-4914119 LC 70-952189
[*PTN 74-4957]

אויף דער שארף פון א רגע.
Korn, Rachel H. 1898-
תל-אביב, המנורה, 1972.

Figure 1. Hebrew title entries, NYPL Research Libraries' catalog. (This represents the beginning of the Hebrew alphabet; columns are read right to left.)

line-printer output on multi-ply paper—1-25 copies
electrostatic reproduction—26-50 copies
offset printing from line-printer output—51-150 copies
offset printing from phototypeset output—151 or more copies.

We tend to think of technological advances only in the more glamorous technologies: greater computing speeds, greater storage densities, more sophisticated CRT displays, etc. Nevertheless, the humble art of printing has been quietly taking advantage of technological developments with lower prices a result. Printing is not a single technology, but many. There are many types of specialty printers, but for the purposes of our discussion we need only note that a difference exists between "short-run" and large-quantity printers. A "short-run" printer specializes in producing fewer than 1,000 copies of a publication, and his equipment is chosen with this in mind. A large-quantity printer uses presses and other equipment economical for large quantities but generally too expensive to handle effectively the job of 200-300 copies. Let us restrict ourselves to the short-run printer. This is generally the regime we find ourselves interested in for library automation products. For the last four years, the NYPL has dealt with such a printer in New York City: Multiprint Inc. Despite increasing costs for paper and labor, they have managed to maintain our costs at a stable level by effecting improvements in the efficiency of their processes. In fact, on several occasions they have managed to *lower* our prices without sacrificing quality. The first such decrease resulted from their use of an electrostatic process for creating paper print plates of the same quality as metal plates produced photographically. Paper plates have a life expectancy of only about 2,500 copies, but this imposes no constraint on us, for we rarely require more than 450 copies. A second price decrease was effected when they developed a semiautomated press, which reduces to a matter of seconds the time required for changing paper plates. The most recent development involves mechanization of the process for creating a matrix of pages for a printing plate for a signature. Ironically, this process involves the use of yet another technology, which may offer the lowest price for hard-copy output: computer output microfilm (COM). The irony lies in the fact that by harnessing this technology, our printer has offered us such an attractive price that we have delayed consideration of a microform catalog for a while longer. The potential is enormous; with a single pass through the photocomposition device we are in a position to produce both low-cost, graphic-quality printed catalogs, and microform catalogs of similar graphic quality. As an added bonus, our costs for the photocomposed copy will be cut in half!

The remainder of this discussion will concern itself with COM. There are two basic kinds of COM: (1) alphanumeric COM—monospace line-printer-like output, and (2) graphic COM—typesetting-quality output. The former is lower in basic price, and requires the least amount of specialized software. Generally, one needs only to redirect the output from a program designed to produce a printed listing on a high-speed printer to a magnetic tape. With modern operating systems this can be accomplished by changing only a single JCL card. As with the rest of the universe, even alphanumeric COM comes in many different varieties. The simplest, cheapest, and most common produces only upper-case output. Upper-case/lower-case capability is now commonly available with the result that character sets are no longer a limitation. Nonetheless, one should exercise care to insure that some of the special characters are available—such as open and close brackets—to avoid unpleasant surprises when the first batch of fiche are delivered.

In the last several years we at NYPL have, in cooperation with two separate vendors (the first is no longer in business), developed a full ALA character set capability for alphanumeric COM. The Library of Congress is developing such a capability with yet a third vendor. Several other vendors have developed greatly expanded character set capability but, to my knowledge, no one else in the United States has developed support for the full ALA set, as an alphanumeric COM option.

Thus, COM can be had, in ascending order of cost for the master copy, with: upper-case only, upper-case/lower-case, a full ALA character set, and graphic-art-quality typesetting. The last is produced by a photocomposition device and thus is available with a virtually unlimited character set and a full range of type sizes and faces. Note well, this ranking by cost represents only the cost for the master copy. Additional copies are made by duplicating the original film, hence the cost of copies is quite independent of the master. As we have already pointed out, graphic-quality output can cut the number of pages, or frames, in half; therefore, the same considerations that apply to printed output are in effect when many copies are to be made.

Before we attempt to consider the relative costs of each type of COM we should first discuss the other variables which can affect cost. COM is available in two basic forms: microfilm and microfiche. Both are available in various reduction ratios. In deciding between film and fiche, one must consider the cost of the associated reader. A typical microfiche reader can be obtained for under $160, while a comparable motorized film reader will cost about five times as much (about $800). The basic cost for creating film and fiche is about the same per frame. Cassette or cartridge microfilm must be loaded into holders at a cost of about $2.00 per cassette. In the most popular size of film—16mm—only about 1,800 frames can be loaded into a cassette. This adds about .1 cent to the cost of each frame/copy, which is significant in the domain of prices associated with microforms.

Differences in reduction ratio do affect the cost of a fiche master, but only slightly. The major effect occurs in the cost of multiple copies. There seem to be no real standards for microforms; therefore, depending on the reduction ratio and the COM vendor's ingenuity and cooperation, various numbers of frames can be placed on a single fiche. Because the cost of making copies depends only on the number of fiche, the number of frames on a fiche can be quite significant in determining the total cost of a complete list in multiple copies. The 42X fiche format seems to be reasonably standardized. A single fiche will normally hold 208 frames, one of which is reserved as an index to the individual frames. On the other hand, 24X fiche are available in a wide variety of grid layouts. This is probably due to the existence of both COM and source document microforms at that reduction ratio. Source document microforms are made by photographing a printed page, normally 8½ X 11 inches, whereas COM is generally created in the proportions of computer printout, nominally 11 X 14 inches. At NYPL we have been using a 7 X 10 arrangement of frames for our 24X fiche (this means 69 frames of data plus one frame for an index). Higher reduction ratios are also available, such as 48X which permits 270 frames/fiche. As you can see, by choosing the appropriate reduction ratio, significant reductions in the cost of multiple copies can be achieved. Furthermore, a format which reduces the number of fiche simplifies refiling the fiche after use.

Microforms obviously cannot be read with the unaided eye, so some simple form of indexing must be provided. In this respect microfiche are far superior to microfilm. There are techniques for indexing microfilm, but none are totally satisfactory. The simplest techniques rely on an odometer built into the film reader. These are usually not very accurate, but the index can get you close enough to permit you to scan further. Other techniques rely on special frames placed at alphabetic breaks, with distinctive markings at fixed positions on the frame. When the film is passed through the viewer at high speed, the markings appear as a distinctive pattern on the screen. An index affixed to one edge of the screen allows one to determine at a glance approximately where he/she is in the alphabet. Probably the best technique developed yet for public use is that provided by the Information Design and Autographics readers. They simply have a set of gears connected to the film transport mechanism, which are used to drive a cursor. The cursor acts much like the pointer on an FM radio dial. In this case, instead of pointing to the tuning frequency in response to a twist of the dial, it points to entries in a printed index in response to the film's motion; *ergo* one knows where he or she is on the film. This technique, although promising, is still subject to some mechanical problems. It also shares the limitations of odometer indexes; they can only specify film position to within approximately one hundred frames.

Microfiche can be indexed much more precisely, and in addition eliminate awkward sequential searching. Time spent in moving film while searching for the correct frame is obviously unproductive time. In addition, most users find this quite irritating. More generally, film may be likened to a sequential data set, while a set of fiche are more closely analagous to a direct-access file.

Most service bureaus producing microfiche generally employ a preprocessor to index the fiche automatically. If the program that creates the listing is designed to create dictionary headings on each page, or if a data element in a specified position on the page can be used for this purpose, the service bureau can automatically provide an index. The vendor will usually provide two levels of index: (1) some frame of the fiche is chosen as the index frame (it will contain the dictionary heading for each frame on the fiche with a reference to the coordinates of that frame): and (2) a higher level index can also be provided (this simply consists of the dictionary heading of the first frame on the fiche in large, eye-readable characters across the top of its fiche). When the fiche are arrayed in front of a user, he or she can select the correct one with the unaided eye from the eye-readable heading. When that fiche is loaded into the reader, the index frame will give the location of the desired frame. As the reader moves the cursor to the specified coordinates, the correct frame is displayed on the screen. This can usually be accomplished in less time than it would take a reader to leaf through a printed volume. The fiche vendor will also provide an additional service: each fiche will be sequentially numbered with eye-readable characters. This greatly facilitates refiling the fiche after use.

I regret that I cannot give you a single figure that represents the cost of COM output, nor a simple formula which will permit you to make a choice with some feeling of confidence. The number of parameters involved is just too great. I can, however, discuss some of the parameters involved and the effects of varying them. I have thus far been talking only about alphanumeric COM. The basic costs associated with this depend on the options chosen: (1) upper-case/lower-case fiche, at 42X reduction—prices average about two cents/frame; (2) full ALA character set, at 42X reduction—only two vendors currently provide this service, with respective prices of 4.5 and 9.3 cents/frame (Figure 2 shows a portion of the character set as developed for COM); and (3) copies of 42X fiche—about 0.1 cent/frame.

Thus, a 750-page listing produced in 100 copies with an upper-case/lower-case character set would cost about $116.60—less than the cost of paper needed for seventeen copies! Note that four fiche are required for this list, and that the last fiche will be only about one-half full. Nonetheless, you would normally be charged as if they were full for both the master and for each copy. If the same listing were produced with a full ALA character set, it would cost about $177.00. Note that although the master is nearly five times as expensive, the total bill is increased by only 50 percent. This is the result of a simple fact that is easy to overlook: the cost of duplicating many copies is more significant in determining the total price than is the cost of the master.

Let us consider one simple variation. Let the fiche be created with an

Figure 2. A portion of an ALA alphanumeric COM character set

ALA character set, at 48X. The price of the 100 sets would then be about $150.04. This is 15 percent cheaper than if produced at 42X. There are other variations one might wish to consider. For example, without great difficulty a vendor can provide frames proportioned according to one reduction ratio, with characters at a lower reduction, and slightly greater space between lines. This helps improve legibility and if accented characters are to be used, reduces the probability that descenders or ascenders will interfere with diacritics. At NYPL we currently produce 42X fiche with 38X characters. In order to do this, we must limit the number of characters on a line and the number of lines per page, which in turn increases the number of frames needed for a listing. The net result is an increase of 36 percent in the number of frames. The effect on our hypothetical 750-page list would be to increase the COM price from $177.00 to $221.25, as we would now need five fiche. Although the fractional difference is large, the absolute difference is quite small. We have found the increased legibility and user satisfaction to be worth the difference in price.

These calculations could be carried out *ad nauseum*. The important point is that the number of options are limited only by your, and your service bureau's imagination. At any rate, we should now have enough information to establish another crossover point: the range of copies for which microfiche represents the optimal medium. I shall not attempt to do this for you, as the crossover point is too dependent on the size of the listing and its publication frequency. The reason for this dependence is quite simple: in the price of each frame of each copy we must include the amortization of the price of the reader. I believe you now have enough data to do this calculation yourself.

I should like to conclude by discussing what I consider to be the most interesting recent COM development. As I mentioned earlier, a photocomposition device can be used to produce microfilm. Information International Incorporated (III) manufactures and supports three of the most sophisticated photocomposition devices: the Videocomp 800, the COMp80, and the FR60. All three machines are capable of producing 16mm and 35mm film; the COMp 80 can also directly create microfiche. The NYPL has been experimenting with 35mm Videocomp output, which can then be put through another photographic process (developed by NCR) to create ultrafiche. This technique is attractive in that no significant software modifications are necessary. In fact, the only change of any magnitude involves the creation of an indexing frame. More important, we can have access to all of the type fonts we use in our printed book catalogs and can thus use all of the type-face and type-size differences to convey information. We can also display non-Roman-alphabet vernacular text; our Hebrew character font will be available on the COM device.

Because of two physical limitations, the full benefits of photocomposed ultrafiche cannot be derived yet: (1) reduction by a Videocomp is fixed, as is second-stage reduction in the NCR process; and (2) a Videocomp restricts the frame size on microfilm output to the equivalent of a 7 X 9 inch full-size page. We are actively seeking solutions to both of the problems. We are also carefully following the progress being made by LC in its use of the COMp80 family of hardware. In fact, it was LC's early attempts to produce the subject-heading guide on a Videocomp in ultrafiche that provided the impetus for our own explorations in this direction.

Even with the limitations just mentioned, we have determined that we could reduce the cost of our supplements to 28 percent of our current printing prices by producing them in photocomposed ultrafiche. This would mean that we could capitalize 250 readers, with the expected savings realized in less than two years. If we assume that one-fifth of all readers would have to be replaced each year, then it would take nearly three years to capitalize the readers and to begin deriving benefits from this technique. As I pointed out, our printer has made our printing prices so attractive that now we can only expect to save 53 percent by converting. This sounds like a substantial saving, but at this rate it would take more than four years to capitalize the cost of 250 readers.

The fractional savings would be roughly equivalent if we also converted the cumulation to microform, but the absolute savings would be twice as great. Therefore, even with our new lower printing prices, we could expect to capitalize the new readers and replacements in approximately three years—but this is still not the complete picture. Consider again just a microform replacement for the printed supplements. They consist of four volumes each produced in 250 copies; in theory, we can thus provide 1,000 service points. It does not seem that we would in fact need that many readers; nonetheless, we would probably need more than 250. This factor would dramatically change much of the foregoing arithmetic.

The nearly 40 percent reduction in printing costs has permitted us adequate margin to await and evaluate further developments for at least another year or two. This additional time can prove extremely valuable at this juncture. We can simultaneously closely observe developments in CRT and communication costs during this period. This will permit us to extrapolate more reliably their trends before we make a large investment in microform reading equipment. Nonetheless, it must not be forgotten that two-thirds of the 40 percent reduction in our printing costs is directly attributable to photocomposed microfilm.

In conclusion, developments in display technology are dramatically altering both the economic and service potentials of automated library systems. Microforms are providing some of the most fertile developments in this revolution; many of these benefits can be enjoyed immediately, and current trends promise even more exciting developments in the near future. Decision-making, alas, is made extremely complex—not because of limitations, but rather because of a cornucopia of very attractive options.

About the only absolute statements which can be made are: (1) the effectiveness and viability of automated information systems are inextricably linked to the economics of display media, and (2) recent developments although varied and in a state of extreme flux, seem very promising.

Appendix

1. Multi-ply Paper vs. Xerox

P = cost of printing on page containing 55 lines, @ 300 lines/minute, @ $45.00/hr.

P = (55 X 45.00) = .1375

Cm = cost of *n* multi-ply copies

Cm = print time + paper

= 1/4 (.1375 + .0365) n = .0435n

Cx = cost of *n* electrostatic copies

Cx = cost of print time + 1 part paper + xeroxing

Cx = .1375 + .0091 + .038n = .146 + .038n

Cm > Cx

.0435n > .146 + .038n

$$n > \frac{.140}{.0055} = 25.4$$

2. Xerox vs. Offset Printing

Cx = cost of Xeroxing

Cx = .038n

Co = cost of offset printing

Cp = cost of plate + cost of copies

Cp = 1.82 + .003n

Cx > Co

.038n > 1.82 + .003n

$$n > \frac{1.82}{.035} = 52$$

3. Offset Printing from Line Printer Output vs. Offset Printing from Phototypeset Output

Characters on a line-printer page—57 lines X 132 characters/line = 7524

Characters on a phototypeset page—8½ X 11″ with 3/4″ margins provides 7 X 9½″ print area.

7 X 9½″ = 504 pts. X 684 pts.

Number of 8 pt. lines on page—684/8 = 85.5 ≈ 86

Number of characters/line—on the average, an 8 pt. character occupies 4 pts. horizontally, therefore,

504/4 = 126 char/line

Characters/page = 10,836

R = page reduction

$$R = 7{,}524/10{,}836 = .694$$

$$Co = 1.82 + .003n$$

Cp = cost of offset printing from photocomposed output

Cp = (cost of photocomposition + cost of plate + cost of copies) X reduction ratio.

$$Cp = (1.00 + 1.82 + .003n)R = (2.82 + .003n)(.694)$$

$$= 1.96 + .002n$$

$$Co > Cp$$

$$1.82 + .0030n > 1.96 + .0021n$$

$$n > \frac{.14}{.00091} = 153$$

INDEX